Keep Moving Forward

By Matt Landry

KEEP MOVING FORWARD

Other titles by Matt Landry:

Forward, Upward, Onward

Casting Your Troubles into the Grand Canyon

Your Road Map to Happiness

INTRODUCTION

"One day, the mountain that is in front of you will be so far behind you, it will barely be visible in the distance. But the person you become in learning to get over it? That will stay with you forever. And that is the point of the mountain"

-Brianna Wiest

The call of the mountains is hard to explain. Some people get it and some don't. It's no different from the call to become a doctor or a glass blower. It may be true for other professions too, I guess. The same often applies to people who have a calling to go to the sea or the desert. Whatever that calling is, it can be intoxicating. More importantly, it can be healing. It's a place we feel at home. A destiny and a destination all wrapped up into one bundle.

John Muir's famous quote, "The mountains are calling and I must go," has become a mantra for so many. We're drawn to the tall places, the wide-open spaces, and the outdoors in general for so many reasons. The scent of pine and dirt, and the lure of rocks and wood. We're finding out what so many have known for years:

nature has the capacity to teach and heal.

After creating our easy lives behind phone screens, televisions, or steering wheels, we're discovering that nature is where our roots lie. We feel better outdoors. To be immersed in nature is, well, natural. It feels right. The sun and fresh air are necessary components to our overall well-being. Both physically and mentally.

"To travel on foot is to travel in the fashion of Thales, Plato, and Pythagoras. I find it hard to understand how a philosopher can bring himself to travel in any other way; how he can tear himself from the study of the wealth which lies before his eyes and beneath his feet."

-Jean-Jacques Rousseau

Exercising outdoors is also known to have countless proven positive effects. It increases blood flow. The fresh air sharpens our senses. Our stress goes down and our serotonin and dopamine levels go up. We feel calm and focused. No wonder that when we're in the midst of the outdoor experience, we feel focused and alive.

To those for whom the call of the mountains is their muse, that call is usually strong. We hike. Our confidence grows, answers to problems and obstacles come easily to us. Our thinking becomes clearer. Our lung capacity and balance improve. We're no longer afraid to become cold, wet, hungry, or dirty. Uncomfortable is a new way of life. We can embrace the suck easier. As we start our journey hiking and conquering, we begin to realize something: We're not actually conquering any mountains or trails. We're simply conquering ourselves.

You see, nature is an incredible teacher.

Sure, life throws obstacles and challenges our way, and we muddle through them. But by creating our own sort of challenges in a controlled way, we're better able to face those challenges and surprises that we all encounter every day.

Picture a favorite teacher from kindergarten or first grade. I assume that in most cases they were gentle, kind, and caring. The teacher was soft-spoken and patient.

Casually walking among the trees and ferns feels very similar to that. It's like a sort of hiking kindergarten. We learn to play nice, not litter, be attentive to our surroundings, and adjust to a different pace and rhythm of life. It's beautiful. I lovingly go back to hiking kindergarten often.

If that casual walk in the woods is like going back to elementary school, then the mountains are much like going for a doctorate degree. Now we're going to college. It's real work. The college instructor pushes those boundaries to see what we're really made of. No more patient and soft-spoken teacher. We've matured. We're no longer kids.

Do we have a first aid kit? Do we know how to navigate in the woods with a map and compass? We learn that we need to leave itineraries behind in case of an emergency. We need to carry rain gear and extra stuff to keep ourselves well. In some rare cases, to keep us alive.

But the simple walks in the woods weren't enough. We needed something harder. We embraced a new challenge. Climbing mountains is real work now. These are harder obstacles we place in our way. Sometimes multiple obstacles. Here's the thing, though: This is where we learn the tough stuff. Endurance, grit, discipline, and discomfort. We've been avoiding this stuff forever. Now it's time to face the crap. It's time to clean out the fridges of our heads of whatever has expired and smells.

In the long run, the hardest climbs in those mountains help us discern what doesn't serve us any longer. It's just us and what we carry out there. Nothing else. We whittled down the packs on our backs to a lighter weight, and we eliminated any unnecessary baggage.

To make us earn that hiking doctorate, the lessons come a little stronger the harder the trail and the taller the mountain. That is to say, the lessons are well earned. They sink in deeper. We're really getting it now. Life, relationships, self-awareness, and so much more.

They all make more sense.

"Comfort zone" has become an overused term these days, but there is a distinct learning experience from stretching it a bit. Sometimes a little bit more and more each day. Oftentimes by climbing a taller and taller mountain, both figuratively and literally.

It would be an understatement to say that the lessons I've learned from my countless hikes have been life-changing. Like many lessons learned, they seemed to come to me only as I matured. I think we all reach a point where life presents itself to us. It unravels its secrets and reveals much of its knowledge and wisdom. In other words, many of the lessons are presented to us when we're ready for them.

This book is devoted to some of those important lessons learned along the way, lessons that were derived from hiking thousands of miles over perhaps hundreds of mountains. With that said, you don't have to be a hiker to enjoy or connect with any of these revelations.

I'll frame each lesson with some hiking-related stories or anecdotes from the past, but the takeaways are just as important to a non-hiker as they are to a hiker. In other words, these are not hiker-exclusive lessons.

I've had the joy of hiking all over the United States. From California to Maine and from South Dakota to Texas. I've sauntered countless trails. Many times I hiked for sheer enjoyment; others, I seemed to be searching. Looking for answers. I'm always in the pursuit of personal growth. The mountains and wilderness always answer those questions. Like any good riddle of what life is really all about, nature reveals these answers if you look hard enough. And in the style of nature, these answers always come slowly and in their own time.

I've often climbed mountains as part of a bigger goal. Sometimes I've chosen a certain peak or route to push my limits. I've done lists of hikes as well. The big goals associated with mountains are slowly fading away, and the lesson portions are now coming to fruition. I hike because it's good for both my mental and physical health. It soothes my soul. I hike because it gives back to me, and as it gives back to me, I'm able to give back to those around me. By making myself a better person, I can make those around me better people as well.

If you hike, many of these lessons will have you nodding your head in agreement. A few are lessons you may have missed. I hope to shine some light on some parts of your hiking journey not yet revealed to you. And who knows? Maybe you'll start looking for many lessons on your own, not realizing the deeper connection that hiking can offer.

Wisdom comes in many forms, and we learn from many sources. Not only were the trails I walked upon able to calm and settle my mind, the people I interacted with taught me so much as well. Hikers are a wonderful community of like-minded souls.

I'll have many points of view and stories from friends who have hiked for years. Their perspectives and anecdotes only add to the breadth of this book. They took on challenges of their own, and I was both inspired and motivated by them.

It wasn't until a few years ago that I started to assemble and sort through many of the lessons I have learned. Most lessons we just take for granted. It isn't until we contemplate what we've learned that we can digest and assemble it properly, I guess.

After releasing *Forward, Upward, Onward*—a book about lessons learned while hiking the forty-eight 4,000-foot peaks of New Hampshire—I started to give talks and seminars related to it. Instead of rehashing old hiking stories or trying to present all forty-eight lessons from that book, I decided to reassemble some of the more important lessons and present those.

The talks were a big hit. As I started to think about my next writing project, *Forward, Upward, Onward, Part 2* came to mind. I started to hike the 4,000-footers again for a second round. The idea didn't appeal much to me, though, for several reasons. I had already done that idea with the first book, and the new lessons weren't as deep. I was having too much fun doing these new (old) hikes, and the write-ups about the peaks were short and cheerful:

"I had a blast."

"Great hike."

"Wonderful weather."

I'm not complaining, mind you, but a book full of that just isn't anything to bite into. I wanted to create a meaningful book. Hence, the idea for this book came to mind. Many of the lessons and stories here have never been publicly brought to light before.

These nine lessons are the most powerful that I've taken from the hikes, the trials, the trails, the tribulations, the celebrations, and the accomplishments.

I hope they resonate with you.

Enjoy.

P.S. - I'm a self-published author, so reviews are crucial to the overall success of this book. If you have a moment after reading it, please consider leaving one.

Much love!

DO IT SCARED

"I've had a lot of worries in my life, most of which never happened."

-Mark Twain

I often say I found much of my confidence from doing things afraid. And let me tell you, many of my hikes scared me a LOT. But most of the fear came beforehand. With trail descriptions that claimed a hike was difficult, rocky, dangerous, or challenging, how could I not be a little concerned? When you start mixing in questionable weather forecasts and more experienced (and faster) hiking partners, it's a mental cocktail for some good, old-fashioned anxiety.

After enough experiences and plenty of restless nights, I was able to better settle into a calmer pre-hike rhythm. After you've faced the tougher days (often more mental than physical), you start to relax. What used to be out of your comfort zone becomes your comfort zone. The walls expand, and what was once frightening is now normal. It doesn't always happen overnight or after doing it once, though. You often need to continue pushing the walls of that comfort zone. Even if it's by sticking your toe out there to start. Even small steps build confidence.

I don't always like the word *confidence*, though.

That word can conjure up a cocky feeling sometimes. It makes you sound like you're ready to conquer the world and everyone in it. Maybe *self-respect* or *life-situation adjustments* are better. For the sake of argument, I'll still use *confidence*, but what I really mean is a truer sense of self. That's what conquering fear does. That's what climbing mountains does. You simply get to know yourself better.

Of course, I obviously didn't conquer any of these mountains. As I've alluded to, I'd like to think that all those mountains and struggles helped me conquer myself instead. Those climbs, long walks, muddy boots, rainy days, and cold mornings added up to me finding myself. Being comfortable in my own skin. Being able to judge others and myself far less. They taught me that by doing things afraid, I was less apt to react poorly to similar situations that everyday life presents. I learned to step forward in ways I previously never thought I could.

I don't want to knock my comfort zone completely. Comfort zones are there for a reason. Nature instilled a reptile-like hardwiring in our brains that helps keep us out of trouble. It used to keep us alive back in the days of predators when we were the prey. Those days are long gone, but our brains don't know the difference. That fight-or-flight pattern that evolved over thousands and thousands of years is still present and doesn't always know the true difference between life and death. That same hardwiring is tribal, which is why we're often scared to fail or embarrass ourselves. We're frightened that the tribe (our family, friends, or community) will judge us. It's a big reason why we're genuinely concerned about what other people will think about us.

We haven't helped matters by creating our own fears. I mean, watch the news or scan the headlines these days. They scream of doom looming on every corner. Let's face it, we eat it up because we keep watching and reading about it. Instead of expanding our capabilities and eliminating fears, we seem to be incubating them. As we do so, our comfort zones start to shrink, and shrink, and shrink. You know, I used to drink out of a garden hose as a kid, walked a mile alone to my first-grade classes, and rode my bike up and down a street lit by street lights when I was eleven years old. I'm surprised I'm still alive. Today, those adventures are less common. We've sheltered ourselves and wrapped our kids in bubble wrap.

"Fear is a reaction. Courage is a decision."

-Sir Winston Churchill

Those of you who read my book *Forward, Upward, Onward* know the story of when I started hiking.

For those who haven't read it, here it is in a nutshell. When I was growing up, there was a flat, easy trail in the White Mountains of New Hampshire that I would often walk. After a few miles, it eventually led to a junction of sorts. It's now called Lincoln Woods. If you continued straight at that junction, you would come to a bridge over a river. That bridge led to a trail called The Wilderness Trail. To the left, just before the bridge, was a short, easy walk to some great waterfalls.

For countless years, I chose to bear left and visit the waterfalls and cascades. I never crossed that bridge over the river. Not even to just step foot on the other side. I mean, it was The Wilderness Trail. It had to be named that for a reason, right?

I guess in my mind, that was where the real adventurers went. The brave, skilled, and courageous. The true explorers and danger-seekers. That was a huge limit for me. That was the end of my comfort zone. Back then, the thought of crossing that bridge frightened me. For lack of any other way to word it, I was scared of what lay beyond. As far as I knew, it was all fire, snakes, spiders, cliffs, bears, and dragons.

I can't blame myself too much, though, because in many ways I was unprepared for what lay beyond that bridge. Both physically and perhaps mentally.

What lay beyond that bridge was several 4,000-foot mountains in New Hampshire. As it turns out, in order to get to them, you need to cross that bridge.

There are forty-eight 4,000-foot peaks in New Hampshire. Many people (including myself) make hiking them all a major goal. To make a long story short, I crossed that bridge on my final 4,000-foot summit hike. The forty-eighth one was Owl's Head. My last peak and celebration consisted of crossing that bridge.

That particular summit was intentional for obvious reasons.

Do you know what I found there, beyond the bridge? The land of unknown terror and suffering? What once was the impossible barrier for me, for so many years?

At the start of the hike, I encountered some struggle, a little confusion, overwhelming feelings, and a touch of anxiety. But when the hike was nearing its conclusion and I was to cross that bridge again—knowing this time what was on the other side—I experienced joy, elation, wonderment, self-respect, gratitude, serenity, and so many other positive feelings.

As it turned out, what lay beyond that bridge wasn't so bad after all. No dragons. No fire and lava. Probably some friendly snakes and harmless bears. It turned out that it was just another mountain to be climbed.

It was an incredibly beautiful mountain and a magical experience. And it was far from the doom and gloom I'd perpetuated in my head.

I heard a great phrase years ago that has stuck with me:

"You can be pitiful, or you can be powerful. You just can't be both at the same time." Whether or not we want to believe it, we choose between pitiful and powerful daily. We've all met people who are pitiful because they choose to be so. We also know people who are powerful because they refuse to defer to pity.

"Courage is being scared to death, but saddling up anyway."

-John Wayne

I'll refer to him a little more in the coming pages, but my friend Randy Pierce, an avid hiker, chose to be more powerful than his circumstances. Randy went blind in his early twenties and didn't let it stop him from living. Was he scared? You bet he was! Who wouldn't be?

He's taken what some may consider a disability and turned it into an ability. He helped establish a charitable organization to help the blind, and he hiked. And he hiked and hiked some more. Oh, and if that wasn't enough, he's run marathons and completed a tough mudder.

Can you imagine what it's like to climb a mountain without sight? That includes river and stream crossings, scrambling on ledges, and feeling your way over boulders. Close your eyes and walk a few feet. Scary, right? Now picture that with rocks, roots, and mud. ALL uphill or downhill. Pretty impressive.

He did all of these things with risk involved, but he cut out as much risk as he possibly could by using a well-trained guide dog, hiking with others, and starting off small. He also did all of this scared. He was scared, but he never stopped doing it.

By doing things scared and paying attention to expanding our comfort zones, we choose to be more powerful. That power propels us forward. By facing what scares us, we quiet the power that fear has and take that power for ourselves. People have said knowledge is power. I agree. Knowing what we can accomplish may be one of the most powerful pieces of knowledge we can obtain.

In order to gain that power, we don't have to get rid of every fear we've ever had all at once. We need to tackle fears one at a time. How does that old question go? How do you eat an elephant? The answer, of course, is one bite at a time.

Along with the notion of doing things afraid, we need to be willing to shed parts of our previous lives. This alone can be frightening. I love the following quote from Andrea Dyktra: "In order to love who you are, you cannot hate the experience that shaped you."

Some of us have been through some pretty bad stuff. Some of the worst things we've experienced can be our most important periods of growth.

After going through several major depressions, I came to the conclusion that they were, in fact, the best things that had ever happened to me. They changed my life. It obviously didn't feel so good while I was going through them, but they are oh so better after the fact. They caused me to grow in ways I never thought possible. I often say that most people grow up in their teens. I grew up when I turned forty.

We have to love the unknown and embrace it. Here's a trick that may help you. On many of the hikes I accomplished, I acted "as if." What do I mean by that? I acted as if I knew what the trail would be like ahead, not really knowing at all. It's kind of like driving a car at night. You can see only what your headlights are shining on. You can see maybe a hundred feet in front of you, but you keep progressing as if everything is going to go as planned. That's the way I hike now: a hundred feet at a time. Heck, ten feet at a time some days. And if something happens along the way, I simply adjust. Then I focus on the next ten feet, and so on. This method eliminates the entire big-picture aspect of the hike. Much like in life, we need to adjust and face things when they are presented to us.

We have only so much control over our daily lives. It's often said that the only permanent thing in life is change. If change is so prevalent, and ultimately guaranteed, then why do we fight it so much? There are simply some parts of life that are left to chance.

"When facing a challenge, ask yourself: What would a stronger, more confident, and even better version of myself do in this situation? When you truly give it thought and get an answer, that's your inner voice talking—and generally a good idea to listen to it."

-Zero Dean

When we act the part, we become the part (sort of like a self-fulfilling prophecy). Another way of facing some fears is to have (or act like) an alter ego. This is incredibly beneficial, especially in areas where we may not excel. As crazy as the notion sounds, by taking on the characteristics of another person (either real or fictional), we can push past our own limitations. I've done this many times with great success. When I didn't think I could push myself any farther on a hike, I channeled people like Sir Edmund Hillary or other great explorers like Lewis and Clark or Ernest Shackleton. All these great men had the odds stacked against them, but they looked fear in the face and moved forward.

They did what they needed to do, and they did it scared. I love the classified newspaper advertisement that Shackleton put out to recruit members of the team that was to explore the South Pole.

"Men wanted for hazardous journey. Low wages, bitter cold, long hours of complete darkness. Safe return doubtful. Honor and recognition in event of success."

That was a man who feared little. At least he gave that impression.

In short, the ship they sailed south on to explore the South Pole (named *Endurance*) got iced in, then was crushed by the surrounding ice and sank. They resorted to eating seals, then eventually their sled dogs. This was not a wonderful situation. They navigated waters in large life boats in almost impossible conditions to arrive on Elephant Island, only to be stranded again. They were stranded for a total of about two years. All this in bitter cold and often wet conditions. Remarkably, nobody died, and through sheer grit and resilience, all were eventually rescued.

If people like that don't inspire or speak to you, then choose someone who does. Are there any current adventurers or hikers out there you look up to? People who have accomplished what you're going for? Go ahead, channel them. Ask yourself "What would _____ do right now?" or "How would _____ handle this?"

"Not knowing the nature of fear, one can ever be fearless"

-Pema Chödrön

Although I'm not looking for honor and recognition after a hike, I am looking for the self-gratification that comes from accomplishment. Channeling Shackleton helps me find that. The brave souls who endured the cold and brutal conditions are not only motivating, they are wonderful guideposts to the experience. My being temporarily uncomfortable for a few hours pales in comparison to the years they endured those brutal conditions. My suffering is a drop in the bucket.

People like Shackleton found that only by risking going too far can we find out how far we can go. Of course, I'm not talking about going to the point that puts us or others in extreme danger, but testing our limits is important.

Let's examine fear for a minute. So what exactly happens when we get scared? We start sweating and shaking, our attention is alerted more, and we're ready for whatever is coming. So what happens when we're excited? Same thing, right?

One of the most important lessons I learned is that fear and excitement are generally the same emotion. Excited or scared? It's your choice. When I was feeling anxious, I would start using the word *excited* more. As time went on, I actually started feeling more excited. All the same jitters and butterflies in the stomach were there, but they were happier jitters. The anticipation was positive. I changed my perspective of what *scared* and *excited* mean.

"Our deepest fear is not that we are inadequate. Our deepest fear is that we are powerful beyond measure. It is our light, not our darkness that most frightens us. We ask ourselves, 'Who am I to be brilliant, gorgeous, talented, fabulous?' Actually, who are you not to be? You are a child of God. Your playing small does not serve the world. There is nothing enlightened about shrinking so that other people won't feel insecure around you. We are all meant to shine, as children do. We were born to make manifest the glory of God that is within us. It's not just in some of us; it's in everyone. And as we let our own light shine, we unconsciously give other people permission to do the same. As we are liberated from our own fear, our presence automatically liberates others."

-Marianne Williamson

I think that many times I chose not to attempt something not because I thought I would fail, but because I thought I would succeed. I was afraid of the extra responsibility and praise that go with success of any kind. And to be clear, when I say *success*, I mean accomplishing a goal, or bettering myself and the world around me, not the celebrity version.

Another way to overcome fear is to realize that your

deepest fears, weaknesses, and shame are often the source of your greatest contribution to the world. I used to play the humility game, almost to the point of shame. I no longer feel that's appropriate. You have an incredible gift to share with the world. We all do. The question is, Are you sharing it?

One of the benefits of going beyond your comfort zone is that you're constantly rewriting the story you tell yourself in your head. I've given a lot of public presentations on these lessons. The first few times were almost paralyzing. I'm an introvert at heart, and the thought of speaking in front of a crowd made me weak in the knees.*

Did you know that, according to a Chapman University Survey of American Fears conducted in 2014, more people would rather die than speak in front of an audience? It was America's number-one fear.

After my third or fourth speaking engagement, I was much better suited for the occasion. I had learned a few lessons and corrected many mistakes. People started asking *me* for advice on public speaking. By pushing through my comfort zone, I had created a new story to tell. I wasn't so afraid anymore because I had some outcomes to go by. I had some experience. I hadn't actually died or exploded right in front of the audience. Nobody got hurt.

One of the most frightening moments I ever had climbing a mountain was on Bondcliff in the White Mountains. Near the summit there's an iconic spot to take a photo. It's almost as though if you don't get that photo, you didn't hike it. I decided that I was going to go for it no matter what. Now, let me explain what this photo opportunity is all about. It's basically a 3-foot flat landing spot that you kind of need to gently hop onto. There's a small gap between the solid land and this sort of rock column. This column has about a 1,500-foot vertical drop on three sides. One slip on the hop, and it's a long, long drop down.

When I got there, I told my hiking partner to get the camera ready (the photo is best taken from a safer spot about 25 yards away). I told him that this was scaring me to death and that the less time I had to spend on this thing, the better.

He got the shot (in it, I'm leaning toward the main land area), I was petrified and probably stood on the spot for only ten seconds. BUT I did it. And I'm grateful for that opportunity. It certainly didn't cure me of my fear of heights, but we all need to start somewhere, right?

I also firmly believe in the balance of comfort zones. Too many so-called gurus will tell you that if you're not in a constant state of comfort zone-breaching, then you're weak or crazy. Nothing could be further from the truth. The only thing that being in a constant state of going out of your comfort zone will give you is a good case of anxiety and panic attacks. Stepping out of your comfort zone is important. But so is being in your comfort zone.

I don't know how many times I made the long drive

out to hike, then sat in the car at the trailhead. I was often petrified at the thought of heading out. I was comfortable in that car. Heck, many days I shut off my alarm clock and never bothered to make the drive. That bed was pretty damn comfortable.

I was disappointed many, many times that I didn't get a specific walk in. But on certain days I also knew enough to listen to my gut and simply rest because that was the best thing for me.

Doing things out of your comfort zone helps you give yourself permission to do so many other things.

"Stop telling yourself you're not qualified, not worthy, or not experienced enough. Growth happens when you start doing things you're not qualified to do."

-Steven Bartlett

Hiking gives you the ability to free your thoughts. The adrenaline and endorphins are keys to clearing your mind. Science has proven that people with ADD or ADHD benefit greatly from exercise because of the dopamine, serotonin, and endorphin increases that come with it. For many mental conditions—including anxiety, depression, and ADHD—there's a lack of these hormones. Decreased hormones play a part in fatigue, stress, and foggy thinking. Exercise helps remove that junk in your head and clears the path for better thought processes and better living.

When we think clearly, we make better decisions, and more importantly, we're able to piece together our lives by thinking things out. We become more aware of our surroundings. Life is less numb and more alive. When I can think more clearly, I become aware of things, like what I'm worried about and why. Then I can easily create solutions. More importantly, I can sift through the junk in my head and make sense of what I'm thinking. Being able to brush off the junk helps clear the space and energy in my mind for better thoughts and, of course, better things to happen in my life.

"My heart is afraid that it will have to suffer," the boy told the alchemist one night as they looked up at the moonless sky. "Tell your heart that the fear of suffering is worse than the suffering itself. And that no heart has ever suffered when it goes in search of its dreams."

-Paulo Coelho, The Alchemist

Life shrinks or expands in proportion to your courage. Think about that for a moment. Your ability to push forward through adversity—or in this case, fear—is perhaps one of the most important lessons you'll ever learn.

So much regret is tied up with not pushing through fear:

"I wish I had asked him or her out on a date."

"I should have started that business when I had the opportunity."

Not asking that person out and not starting that business are fear-based decisions. We can become too paralyzed by fear to make a move. We lean heavily on comfort or, more accurately, we avoid the discomfort that comes with choosing to act.

They say that depression is regretting the past and anxiety is worrying about the future. I've been through major depression twice. When I went through those periods, my biggest enemy was myself. I had an enormous amount of regret. I was also unable to see past where I was to look hopefully into the future. I thought that my mistakes, which had been based on fear, were so incredibly solidified that my future didn't contain hope and beauty.

Of course, I was incredibly wrong. Pulling myself out of my last depression, I vowed to stop seeking comfort so much. I had a difficult time dealing with and assimilating many of my emotions because I had never really known pain. I had avoided it like the plague. In doing so, I never grew.

KEEP MOVING FORWARD

I've often said I grew up when I was forty years old. At fifty-three, I'm loving every day. I'm also making more mistakes, facing more fears, and forcing myself to go through more discomfort than I ever have before. See the correlation there?

Fear is temporary and is essentially made up. Most of my apprehension came before a hike, not necessarily during it. Most of the time, the parts of hiking that did scare the hell out of me lasted only a few minutes.

Have you ever worried about something that never came true? It's almost like suffering in advance. When I finally found myself out on most of those trails, the worry would start to fade.

We obviously need to remain cognizant that accidents can and will happen. Hiking is not exactly a contact sport, but many seasoned hikers have fallen, twisted ankles, gotten hypothermia, or much worse. Many hikers have died doing what they love.

BUT. Many folks I know have fallen down stairs, gotten into car accidents, or slipped on ice. Life is meant to be lived. Even the hikers I know (myself included) who had an accident on the trail would say, "Get back out there." Injuries are rare and not often serious. The odds are with you as long as you prepare properly and choose a hike you're capable of.

THE DESTINATION IS THE JOURNEY

"Everyone wants to live on top of the mountain, but all the happiness and growth occurs while you're climbing it."

-Andy Rooney

I used to teach a photography course. At one point, I'd offer a selection of slides of photos I'd taken, looking for students to critique them. The discussion was meant to help the students improve their own photography. I explained that all the photos were from a recent mountain hike. As we went through the slides, I would present neat images of trees, mushrooms, or leaves taken from unusual angles. I displayed shots of the sky and cloud formations. I would show pictures of shadows cast by ferns, and serene trails surrounded by trees.

We'd determine what we liked or didn't like about each photo. Sometimes it was the overall composition, the color, or the way it was framed. After receiving several compliments and critiques, I'd always ask the same question: "Did anyone notice anything unusual about the photos I took from this particular mountain hike?"

Many would struggle with this question. I'd get a lot of answers like, "Not really, but it looks like you had a great walk."

Invariably, I'd always arrive at the obvious (but apparently not so obvious) conclusion that none of the photos were taken from the summit—the place that supposedly had all the views.

"Oh, yeah, now that you mention it, where are those photos?" many students would ask as it dawned on them that I had, in fact, not supplied the stunning view shot you'd expect.

Many would say, "It was cloudy that day, right? No views? Rain?"

I would always reply that the views were spectacular. But that I'd decided not to showcase those photos because those are the photos that everyone else takes.

What so many fail to notice is the trip up and down the mountain. All the small stuff. That's an entire day of sights and sounds to behold. Most people are so busy rushing up the mountain, looking for the stunning views, that they miss what is right in front of them!

I've taken many wonderful trips. And for some, I left the camera in the car. I did just that on my last trip to the Grand Canyon. Many people said, "I can't wait to see the photos you took." And I disappointed them by explaining that I didn't take my camera.

"Wait. What?" they asked. You're kidding me, right?"

Nope. I simply wanted to enjoy what I was there for: the Grand Canyon. And I did. The Canyon has breathtaking vistas. But instead of trying to reproduce them by taking photos, I wanted to enjoy the sights and sounds just as they were. That experience was much more pleasurable to me during and even after. I still remember more about that trip because instead of tying a visual perspective to it, I had an emotional one.

The summit of any mountain is just another stop along the journey. Many people view it as a final destination. "We made it!" But in fact, then they need to go back down the mountain. And after that, there's potentially another mountain. And another.

Think about people who do longer hikes. That may better represent what I mean. For example, when you hike the Appalachian Trail northbound, after you summit a mountain in Georgia you still have many, many more to go. The journey continues. It doesn't end at a peak. (Well, eventually it does, but you get the picture.)

After I finished climbing the forty-eight 4,000-footers of New Hampshire, my feeling of accomplishment didn't come at that actual final summit. It came when I arrived back at the car. That was when the hike was really finished and the goal was complete. While descending the summit and taking that long walk back, I savored every moment. I knew that the goal was nearing its completion but was still very much in motion.

I realized at a very young age that life is precious and every day is a gift. So I made it a point to travel when I was young and experience life in as many ways and places as I could. I would see people working themselves to death, and I didn't want that for myself. I'm not saying this to sound negative, but I think we all know someone who worked their whole life, then died a year after they retired. Or passed away or got sick just before they retired.

"The antidote to exhaustion isn't rest. It's nature."

-Shikoba

I'm not saying there's anything wrong with hard work. That hard work is a great basis for other events in life, including the monetary expenses it incurs. These adventures cost real money. I'm very proud to say that I have a pretty good work ethic. But we also need to live life, spend time with the ones we love, and "climb that goddamn mountain" (as Jack Kerouac once said).

The office, the lawn, the dishes, and the laundry will still be there when you get back to them. As a matter of fact, there's a saying that warns to be careful how much attention you give work because they'll have a replacement in your job faster than your obituary can get posted.

We live in a fast-paced society. Hiking slows us down—that is, if we let it. (Many would argue that the last several miles of a long hike can seem like forever, but that's not what I'm referring to.)

The more we take the time to look around us and take it all in, the more that time seems to slow down. Hiking and the great outdoors also heighten our senses and trigger the release of crucial hormones that help us focus.

Speaking of focus, whether or not we know it, most of us have probably put our phones and devices away while we walk and climb. The focus is no longer FOMO (fear of missing out), complete with vibrations, notifications, and ringtones. Instead, we have a simpler focus on what's right in front of us. The rest of the world goes away. Our attention is on the top, or the finish, or the beer at the end. Better yet, our focus also shifts to what's right in front of us, begging to be noticed: The trees, sky, rocks, and water. The sounds, sights, and smells of the outdoors. As we progress along our outdoor journey, we find ourselves paying attention to the now. We're mindful and present.

Events in life don't all need to have a huge significance. We've been programmed to think everything has to be like fireworks on the Fourth of July: flashy, quick, and entertaining, with a big bang at the end. Life isn't always like that, though. As a matter of fact, many people, including myself, hike for the opposite effect. I often go walking in the woods to simply walk in the woods. No summits, no views, no waterfalls. The less I'm distracted, the more I slow down. The more I slow down, the more I notice and appreciate.

Many years ago I got caught not being in the moment while hiking Mt. Wachusett, a mountain near my home. I must have had a bad experience at work shortly before that hike, because I put my headphones on, turned the music up full blast, and let my boss have it. Well, kind of. I was having it out with him by myself, on a hiking trail.

At one point I stopped to take a quick break and saw that was a lady right behind me. I'd had no idea she was there. "You totally heard me having a conversation with myself, didn't you?" I said.

"Oh, yeah, for about the last fifteen minutes or so. No worries, though" she said. "I do it all the time as well."

One of the greatest hiking experiences I had was in Vermont many years ago. I wasn't up for any of the big peaks, so I decided to just follow a stream. As simple as it may seem, it was magical. I was off trail but still well within my safety and comfort zone, knowing where I was. I walked in areas that may or may not have been seen by any human before. I hopped from rock to rock and meandered for quite a while. Miles, as a matter of fact. I found a nice, big rock and lay in the sun, listening to the water flow by. The world just went away, but at the same time, I was present with everything around me.

Life made perfect sense.

"The finish line is for the ego. The journey is for the soul."

-Pattie Gonia

I don't necessarily mean this as a religious or spiritual statement, but if it speaks to you as such, please treat it so. I think many of us hike mountains for many different reasons. One reason many may not admit or acknowledge is that it places us in the presence of something bigger than we are. When we walk in a national park, look over something as majestic as the Grand Canyon, or take the time and effort to admire the view from the summit of a mountain, we stand in awe of creation. We take in the beauty before us and realize that we are a part of that beauty. The beauty is also within us.

We begin to understand at a much deeper level that the focus we spend much of our lives on is petty—traffic jams, slow internet, what we should have said to him or her, the insufferable twenty-minute wait in line at the restaurant. It's all petty. It's small potatoes in the grand scheme of things. Hiking provides the big-picture outlook we need to see. Our minuscule problems, in comparison to something like the Grand Canyon, melt away. Time spent in Death Valley or Zion, away from the crowds, is magical. When we sit and look at the stars on a moonless night, we begin to settle into the idea that we're not here on the planet forever and that most of the problems we create in our heads are just useless filler.

I mentioned that when we're in nature, we feel that we're a part of the beauty in front of us. In some ways, I also feel like I'm being watched over and cared for on these walks and hikes. I trust life and have faith that the Universe is somehow looking after me. So many of these hikes have brought me closer to who I am and allowed me to open many new doors while closing countless others. Closure is just as important as new beginnings. As a matter of fact, many new beginnings can't happen without proper closure.

Bringing closure to certain areas of life is healthy and necessary. So are new beginnings. The saying goes that when one door closes, another opens. The question is, Are you continually closing doors without opening new ones? I think many of these doors come across our paths organically. I also firmly believe that we create many of these door-opening experiences and opportunities ourselves. Closure gives us the opportunity to reflect on why some things happened the way they did and the lessons we needed to learn. Some of these lessons take us right back where we began in order to offer a full-circle experience.

Full-circle moments offer so much reflection on our growth. I think these moments are presented so we can see the progress that we've made. When we can see the distance covered in a hike, we can appreciate the journey so much more. On many occasions, I've completed a hike and looked up at the summit from the comfort of the car and thought, *Holy cow. I just climbed that. That's pretty freaking amazing!*

When I slow down, the Universe presents itself to me more plainly. I recognize the signs that it's been sending and the reasons behind things I've gone through. I can also more easily recognize signs for the future. It sounds hokey, but hiking and nature completely bring me back in tune with myself and my surroundings.

"I don't care much for things I can't take with me after I die. Give me love. Moments. Purpose. Things that'll settle in the soul."

-A. R. Lucas

I'd like to reference Randy Pierce again. I wrote about him, the blind hiker, in the last chapter.

Let me fill you in on a few more details about him. He completed the forty-eight 4,000-footers of New Hampshire all in one single winter season. (For those unfamiliar with this feat, it's a monumental task.) He's also done them in summer. This guy helped train former New England Patriot Tedy Bruschi for his hike up Kilimanjaro, for crying out loud! (Which Randy has also hiked.) This is an incredible laundry list of achievements, to say the least.

His lack of sight is not a lack of vision, though. Randy's sight impairment has never stopped him from opening doors for himself, and in turn, countless others.

He has also established a charity to help those with vision disabilities. Most importantly, he inspires through his actions. It's important to him to show what's possible, not impossible. He's not only opening doors for himself, but for countless others. Randy took the time to reassess his life after he lost his sight. He slowed down and got reflective. He found a much greater calling in the process and turned what could be considered a tragedy into a blessing for so many others and—I think even he would admit—for himself.

If you hurry all the time, you rush past all the good things. You need to grab happiness in the passing moments. That's where much of the joy is. Stay open to possibilities. To inspiration. When was the last time you allowed yourself to be inspired by someone else, whether through their art, kind act, ability, or talent?

Are you so strung out on stuff to do that it's become a habit? Just like heroin or cigarettes, work—or, more specifically, keeping busy—can be an addiction. I know people who create meaningless tasks just to stay busy. They don't know how to shut it off. I think we all know someone like that. Usually, their heads work overtime and non-stop. Many keep busy simply to avoid facing past or present traumas.

I suggest we stop the busywork. Life moves quickly, and sometimes we fill it with the mundane chores of everyday life, giving them a disproportionate priority. I know I certainly do. We need to remind ourselves that life is more than our daily to-do lists and the manufactured importance we give to things that don't deserve it.

I've found that hiking is a healthy drug of sorts. But it can become addictive itself while helping control and curb the other addictions we all have—overeating, drinking too much, shopping too much, spending way too much time on social media or video games, and gambling, to name a few.

Do you remember the carefree mindset you had as a child? I think most of us had little anxiety, and our creative imaginations ran wild. In many ways, we forget what it was like to be eight or nine years old.

Two great hikes have reminded me of what being a kid was like. They were both in winter in New Hampshire. For those of us who grew up in colder climates, snow was a playground. Snow forts, snow days, and snowsuits (remember those?). How about bread bags on our feet for waterproofing? Seems like compared to all of today's fancy technology, bread bags still did a better job.

The first of those experiences occurred on Mt. Potash

in New Hampshire—a great little mountain with a 2,000-foot elevation gain and a good payoff for relatively little effort. The trails were covered in snow but hard from foot traffic. As I was climbing, I heard two people screaming around the corner. I quickly jumped to the side as a blur came at me, then passed me. A few moments later, I heard two women roaring with laughter.

Well, it was two ladies flying down the mountain on a sled. They were both in their early seventies, and their laughter was simply infectious. They apologized for disrupting my hike, but I was anything but upset. I was beaming a smile from ear to ear from the joy they had projected. They remembered what it was like to be a kid, and they had recaptured the essence of carefree childhood.

The second experience was on Mt. Monadnock in Peterborough, New Hampshire. I was hiking with a friend, and we decided to take a less-beaten path down the mountain. Not only was the trail not broken out, but there were snowdrifts everywhere. Time and time again, we trounced through the thick, fluffy snow, sending it flying with every step. I felt like I was eight years old again and playing in the snow. (Although my legs and back didn't feel eight years old the next day.)

So often we chase after happiness and contentment. But if we just relax a little and stay open to the idea, happiness comes poking its head around the corner like a curious cat. Let happiness find you. Nothing soothes the soul like a walk in nature. I find that on these walks, contentment will often flutter right to me like a butterfly and land gently on my shoulder.

Be open to inspiration. You can find it anywhere—even in the bad. When I was going through my last major depression, I would repeat the mantra, "This will be the best thing that ever happened to me." I promise you that it didn't feel like the best thing that ever happened to me when I was going through it. But that mantra was also a major factor of how I got through that depression. Not only did it offer hope, it changed my perspective about the whole thing. It also happened to be the truth. In many ways it was the best thing that ever happened to me.

We need to approach life as if it were a banquet or a fully stocked buffet. In most cases, we are limited only by our imaginations. I've come to the conclusion that when we slow down, all questions are eventually answered. However, we need to listen and look for those answers.

How do you do that?

You slow down.

I guess that some things in life we decide, and some things in life we discover.

BE GRATEFUL AND BE MINDFUL

"I would maintain that thanks are the highest form of thought; and that gratitude is happiness doubled by wonder."

-G. K. Chesterton

I wrote a book on happiness and did hundreds of hours of research. Would you like to know what the biggest factors influencing your happiness are? I'll save you the $14.99 and give you the top three (in order):

1. Being grateful for what you already have (even if you're striving and dreaming for more)
2. Spending time and money on shared experiences (versus buying stuff)
3. Having a purpose to your day

Simple as that!

Well, kind of. There's obviously much more to being overall content and happy than that, but those three factors are essentially the basis for everything else.

And by gratitude, I don't mean thinking that you're better off than others. I'm not always a fan of the "someone has it worse than you" mentality. In many ways, where we are mentally has a lot to do with the choices we make mentally. Someone will always have it worse than us. But that doesn't give us an excuse to be glad about it.

The gratefulness I'm talking about comes from your own heart, regardless of the circumstances you may be in. Because the struggles that you mislabel as bad luck or karma often turn out to be the liberating forces that cause you to grow or change.

As I'll explain in a chapter coming up, the struggles in life are so important. Part of being grateful is appreciating all of it—not just the good stuff. You need to appreciate the struggle too. As I mentioned earlier, the struggle does suck. It's not for the weak. But it should still be appreciated for what it is: a lesson. That lesson could very well include patience, humility, grace, or anger management. And trust me, those aren't easy lessons to swallow.

"These are the good ol' days"

-Carly Simon

During the course of my last major depression, I had the foresight and maturity to keep uttering the words "When this is over, this will be the best thing that ever happened to me." That affirmation was very, very hard to wrap my head around and get out of my mouth some days. Depression can be an incredibly dark and lonely place. A terrifying blackness of the soul.

Maybe it was the mantra that carried over to my realization, but I still say that particular episode of depression was, in fact, the best thing that ever happened to me.

My forced, but well-informed mindset about the situation made it tolerable.

I am incredibly grateful to my depression for the lessons it taught me, for the lengths it made me go to in order to discover myself better, and for the valuable wisdom it imparted about the value of service to others. Discovering how to get out of my own head by teaching, leading, and caring for others was life changing.

I can really appreciate all that the trail has offered me. I certainly have a much different attitude when I walk now. I'm incredibly grateful for the people I've met, hiked with, and spent time with on the trail. I'm grateful for the quality time spent alone, sorting out my thoughts and quieting my brain. I'm grateful for the new socks and fresh shirt waiting for me back at the car after a hike, and for the cold summit beer on a warm day and the big, greasy meal (commonly known as the hiking hangover meal) at the end.

I'm grateful for the serotonin and endorphin rush I get

from the exertion a great hike demands.

I mean, why would a walk in the woods or up a mountain possibly bother me anymore? I'm doing what I love. I'm doing what's good for me.

These are the small yet major things that get me up and out the door They get me to climb when weather is less than perfect, and they help me reach the summits when I may not otherwise feel like doing it.

This gratitude is based on the perceived value that all these things add to my life. As a result, I've come to appreciate the many things that make my life more valuable.

We take most things for granted. We expect that good friends should always be there, or the good job will never go away. We believe that the ones we love will live forever. These are also the very things that we need to be grateful for, because as much as we'd like them too, they won't last forever.

You can be satisfied with less than you think. When you act with gratitude, you can still strive for more, but at the same time you can be happier with what you already possess, the experiences you've had, and the people who surround you.

As I mentioned in the beginning of this chapter, attitude is a great basis for happiness. It offers the building blocks of contentment. Those who are most pleased with life in general are usually the most grateful.

So when are we least happiest? Let's examine that for a moment.

We generally have the least contentment when we are the least satisfied with our lives. That may sound obvious, but think about it for a moment. We are least pleased with life when we least appreciate who and what we are.

We are generally in a state of "things could be better." We're displeased with the way we think life has approached us. We aren't happy with ourselves or anything around us. The more miserable we are, the less likely we are to be thankful for anything.

Happier people also tend to have a growth mindset. For them, a common response in the face of difficulty is, "What is this trying to teach me?" or "What is the purpose behind this?"

For many of the richest people in the world, money was actually not their driving purpose. Their purpose was waking up and jumping out of bed to attack the day. They had a goal in mind: to be successful at their day. The money usually came after. Plenty of wealthy individuals lost it all, got back up, and started all over again. It was their mindset that drove them.

As we speak, I'm sitting on a plane headed for the Southwest. I'd envisioned the flight being a quiet time to reflect and write. I thought that maybe I'd even sit next to an empty middle-row seat. (We all know about the dreaded middle-row seat.) The reality was that I was on a nearly full flight and sitting next to a talkative person with heavy perfume. She slept so soundly that I thought she may have passed away. At one point, she fell asleep holding a cup of ice water and ended up spilling it all over her lap. She never even flinched. She had a book open to the same page for the entire four-hour flight.

I was frustrated, disappointed, and a bit concerned. Then, as I've done at other points in my life, I had to ask myself, *What is this trying to teach me? What lesson can I extract from all of this? What is my attitude right now? Will it bring me aggravation, or will it bring me calm wisdom in the end?*

When I just mindfully shifted my focus, the frustration began to subside.

As it turned out, she was heavily medicated for anxiety, and we struck up a wonderful conversation when she awoke. Plus, she was a hiker. I'd thought my expectations for the flight had been shattered, but instead they'd only been adjusted. I was grateful that my seat neighbor gave me the opportunity to practice mindfulness and self-control. I was also grateful that she revealed a number of fantastic hiking spots that I had overlooked in the Southwest. She offered something that I didn't have before I met her.

I combine being grateful with being mindful because they are interwoven. I think they hold so many similarities. I believe being grateful requires being mindful and fully aware of our surroundings and circumstances. So much joy and peace are missed because we don't take the time to pay attention. Or maybe it's not so much that we don't take the time, but that we forget to pay attention to all of it around us.

"Enjoy the little things, for one day you may look back and realize they were the big things."

-Robert Brault

We have so many opportunities to bless or be blessed, inspire or be inspired, awe or be awed.

The world, and specifically nature, is so awe inspiring. From the simple clover to the majestic mountain, it can blow your mind if you let it.

A common phrase in the hiking world is "getting high." It doesn't mean taking drugs, though. It's a reference to the elevation of a mountain. We can often get the same euphoric feelings from climbing a mountain that other people get from taking drugs. Drugs give some people a way to escape from reality. Hiking a mountain or spending some serious time in nature can often do the same thing.

It's important to note that facing our demons is

imperative. Getting out into nature helps us organize our thoughts so we can slay the dragons of life. Sometimes we need to quiet the mind so we can start making sense of things. A quieter mind can see a bigger picture. And that lets us recognize things for what they are, not what we think they are.

By noticing the small awe-inspiring intricacies of nature, we can also gain the perspective that maybe, just maybe, we concern ourselves a little too much with things that really aren't that big a deal or worry about things that don't really matter.

Practicing mindfulness can be difficult, what with so much grabbing at our attention. But by sauntering in the green of the forest or the reds and browns of the desert, we learn to slow our mental pace and stop looking for what "can be" and start looking for what "is." We focus on what's in front of us more, and that teaches us to do it more frequently in everyday life.

The question I ask myself now is, *What can this teach me?* I ask it quite often.

As a hiker, I'm in a constant state of improvement. I no longer take hiking for granted. I have the ability to get into nature, and I realize that isn't the case for everyone, sometimes, including myself.

Years ago, I hiked Mt. Monadnock with a friend for a glorious sunset. Monadnock is a bustling mountain. It's often cited as the most hiked mountain in the world. You can imagine the size of the crowds at the summit on sunny weekends. There have been times when I've climbed the mountain, seen how busy the summit was, and simply turned around.

On this particular night, though, we had the summit all to ourselves. It was unusual and magical.

Unfortunately, on the way down, I suffered a pretty bad ankle sprain—my first in twenty-five years, actually. Was I upset? Quite the contrary. I was grateful that I could still hobble down without assistance. I was grateful that I still got to experience a wonderful sunset on an empty summit. The sprain had me laid up for about a month. I was also grateful at that point that I would be able to hike again. When I returned to walking in nature, I was far more appreciative that I could do that again.

You never know how much you'll miss something until it's gone.

My hikes these days are steeped in gratitude. I still have some casual hiking goals to complete, but I have no more lists to accomplish. I hike for sheer enjoyment now. Whether it be a major peak or a walk around the local state park, it's all good. It's all nature at its finest.

"It's a funny thing about life, once you begin to take note of the things you are grateful for, you begin to lose sight of the things that you lack."

-Germany Kent

We bounce and bound through all kinds of emotions. Anger, sadness, joy, shame, guilt, elation, anxiety. This is just a short list. I mentioned earlier that I love the saying, "You can be pitiful or you can be powerful, but you can't be both at the same time." That means that you generally can't feel two opposing thoughts or feelings at once.

To take this concept one step further, I think there are really only two emotions, and all the others are subcategories that fall under one of those two.

The two categories are love and fear.

I think any emotion we traditionally think of as "good," like happiness, joy, comfort, etc., are in the love category. The "bad" ones (which aren't all bad, by the way) fall under fear. These would be anger, hate, resentment, jealousy, etc.

When we focus on the love side of emotions, there's little room for the fear-based ones.

One of the biggest love-sided emotions, besides love itself, is gratitude.

"The heart that gives thanks is a happy one, for we cannot feel thankful and unhappy at the same time."

-Douglas Wood

I love the mountains so much because we lack so little out there. And I think that's true for many other people. We're all hooking onto the fact that we can be happy and live comfortably with way less than we thought possible.

When we strip away all the somewhat useless, real-world pressures we put upon ourselves—bills, traffic, social media, or even our jobs—we relax. When we relax, I think we arrive at a natural state of gratitude.

But gratitude for so many, including myself, can be fleeting in moments.

These moments of gratitude are wonderful, but have you ever considered practicing gratitude when things aren't so good? It's not as easy, but it's a good way to live.

I knew a lady years ago who adhered to her faith

stronger than anyone I knew. For her, everything was "God's will." I'm not a religious person, but I love the attitude that the Universe is somehow taking care of us and that even the bad stuff is all for our good. Even when things are difficult, it can help to consider that maybe there's a lesson we need to learn today. Or maybe something in our future requires that we go through what we're going through now.

Our strength eventually swallows our pain. Our fears start to look smaller when we take away their power, and the struggles we go through don't look so bad when we look at the Milky Way on a moonless night in the Grand Canyon.

These are all based upon maturity and gratitude.

EXPECT THE BEST, PLAN FOR THE WORST

"The measure of intelligence is the ability to change"

-Albert Einstein

I chose this lesson for the book because its value goes beyond the obvious planning that goes into a hike. It's just as important to make decisions based on the whole picture. This was and still is a very important concept in my life. Hiking has taught me to prepare for whatever may come my way while being flexible enough to adjust or change as needed. We never stop evolving.

Appalachian thru-hikers, especially inexperienced ones, tend to pack too much. A lot of little things don't seem like much when you're stuffing them in your pack, but when you're carrying them, they certainly add up.

A few years ago, I hiked to the bottom of the Grand Canyon and camped overnight. I obviously needed to take all the supplies needed for the trip, including a sleeping bag and tent. Those had some weight, but it was all the smaller items—DSLR camera, toothbrush, and extra flashlight, just to name a few—that really weighed the pack down. There's being prepared, but there's also such a thing as being over-prepared. It's important to know the difference, both on the trail and in life.

The pack felt heavy going down. But I felt like I was carrying a piano on the way back up. The hike itself was challenging, but the extra weight was brutal.

"I am prepared for the worst, but hope for the best."

-Benjamin Disraeli

We do the same thing in life. A friend is worried or hurt, so we take on some of that burden. We had a tough childhood, so we carry some of that baggage. We encounter people who are negative or abusive, and we continue to interact with them because either we have a history with them or they somehow feel comfortable. It's sort of like that favorite shirt that we keep wearing even though it's practically in tatters.

There comes a time when we need to let go of all the extra baggage in our lives. Much of what we hang onto no longer serves us in any meaningful fashion.

An incredibly important sort of sub-lesson in this main lesson is to pack effectively, but pack light.

This from a NOVEMBER 14, 2008 article in Outsider magazine, titled "Pack Man: The Appalachian Trail Guru", referring to Winton Porter. Winton is a gear guru at Mountains Crossing. A hiking gear store located just 30 miles from the southern start of the Appalachian trail. Porter sees many new or first-time hikers come through and offers advice and suggestions for lowering pack weight. Going through and assessing the pack is referred to as a shakedown.

> *Nobody walks by Mountain Crossings without stopping. The combination hostel and gear store and hiker aid station, at Walasi-Yi in northern Georgia, sits quite literally on the Appalachian Trail. It's the first outpost of civilization that northbounders encounter—and the last for southbounders. Each year, up to 2,000 thru-hikers drop in. Some just pause for the few minutes it takes to grab spare batteries and a Clif Bar. Many linger for a hot shower and a soft bunk and to soak up the history of a lodge that was established in 1937, the same year as the AT itself. Others have no choice but to stop.*

> *Porter makes no judgments. He's seen it all while dissecting the innards of thousands of packs during Shakedowns. Serafin's backpack presents no surprises to Porter—but provides plenty of opportunities to save weight and bulk.*

> *"You want to ask yourself, What does each piece of clothing do for me? Does it insulate? Does it stop wind? Does it stop rain?" he says. "Nylon zip-off pants*

don't do any of those three. If you wear a pair of nylon running shorts over lightweight long underwear, now you have pants that weigh 3.5 ounces instead of two to four times as much."

Each Shakedown session typically nets 12.5 pounds in weight saved. But some yield far more.

.

A pound here and a pound there, and before you know it you're up to four tons, which is the weight of discarded equipment Mountain Crossings ships back home for thru-hikers every year. Porter's pretty certain that UPS uses the Mountain Crossings route to haze new drivers. Another 1,000 pounds in food ends up dumped in the hostel's "hiker box."

Four tons of unneeded gear weight. 1,000 pounds of food. Every year.

And that's just the folks who got their packs assessed.

"By failing to prepare, you are preparing to fail."

-Benjamin Franklin

A little extra weight affects everything from the back to the knees to the neck. The mental baggage we carry around can be just as damaging. It can affect confidence, stress levels, sleep, and productivity.

KEEP MOVING FORWARD

Preparation is essential to a successful journey, which is why I think we often overpack or overthink. We always think that we'll need this or that. With proper assessment, we can often whittle down our packs and our minds, though.

By planning a little more carefully and taking what we need and letting go of what isn't really necessary, we can lighten our loads both on the trails and in our lives.

YOUR ATTITUDE DETERMINES YOUR ALTITUDE

"Attitude is everything, so pick a good one."

-Wayne Dyer

Let's cut right to the chase on this one. When I'm talking about attitude, I'm really talking about mindset. I'm talking about being self-aware.

I'm referring to the choices we have and the choices we make when we react to the world around us. And yes, they are all choices.

"Self-awareness is the key to transformation. The more aware you are of your thoughts, feelings, emotions, and actions, the easier it is to make the changes and improve your reality. Look within, be real with yourself, take responsibility for your energy, connect with your divine truth and look at life through the eyes of love and compassion."

-Carrie M. Bush

Many may not agree, but it's up to us how we react to the people and circumstances around us and to life in general. Other people don't make us happy. The traffic isn't what angers us. And our career isn't what makes us frustrated. We are the source of all those feelings. Those things may all be triggers that lead us to a certain choice in our reactions, but ultimately, we choose those reactions.

Most people are skeptical about this, but it's the truth. The sooner we accept this, the easier life gets.

Should there be times when we choose to be angry, happy, or frustrated? Absolutely! I'm not saying we shouldn't feel these emotions. I'm just saying that whether we know it or not, we choose them.

Now, in all fairness, we probably select these emotions without even knowing it. Some of it is genetic, but much of it is a reaction that we've been programed to have. Parents and teachers taught us how to respond to events, and the rest consists of our repeated actions and reactions.

There may have been a triggering event that pushed a certain belief to the forefront for you, either good or bad. Now every time it rains or you see a yellow house, it evokes a reaction. Maybe that yellow house reminds you of spending happy times at your grandmother's house. Maybe the rain represents your traumatic first day of school in second grade.

Part of conditioning your mindset is adjusting your

thoughts around triggers. The rain is the rain, and it holds no personal grudges against you. And a yellow house isn't inherently good just because it's yellow.

The traffic is also just there. It isn't backed up on purpose just to tick you off. It's just traffic.

Climbing mountains has helped me immeasurably with the process of choosing my emotions and reactions. The long slogs in the mud and rain come as joyful times to me now. But they didn't always. I needed to slog enough times to realize that the hike would occur either way, mud or no mud. I can choose to smile or I can choose to be miserable. It's my choice.

It's easier to realize that these are choices when I create an almost premeditated scenario. I kind of put myself out there to force myself to choose what reactions I want to have.

Hiking is a learned experience not only in pre-determined suffering, but also in adjusting your mindset.

Sure, you can argue that being outdoors and away from the hustle and bustle of life is bound to be enjoyable. But there's still an enormous element of mindset involved in so many hikes.

"No pessimist ever discovered the secrets of the stars, or sailed to an uncharted land, or opened a new heaven to the horizon of the spirit."

-Helen Keller

Here's kind of my definition of mindset in a nutshell. I'm borrowing a little of this from *Forward, Upward, Onward.*

Have you ever taken a trip on a plane on a cloudy day? Maybe it was foggy or drizzly in the morning. You boarded the airplane and took off with little to no visibility. First there's thick fog. Then, all of the sudden, you pop out above the clouds, and the sky is clear and the sun is shining brightly.

When you rise above the clouds, the sun appears. The lesson is that the sun is actually always there. It's always shining. Sometimes it's just obscured by the clouds.

On many great hikes, it can be tough to judge if you're going to get a view on a cloudy day. More than once I've hiked in the thick fog or drizzle, only to pop my head out of the clouds to catch a stunning undercast on a summit. The sun is always out. Always. Sometimes the clouds are just in front of it for a little while.

I've learned many attitude and mindset lessons from

those around me. So many have endured so much. Those people inspire me. One is my friend Chris.

On one trip, with no lists still in mind, I decided to do two hikes with two old friends, Ike and Pierce (Mount Eisenhower and Mount Pierce), in the White Mountains of New Hampshire. Chris joined us. I had hiked both 4,000-foot peaks several times before, but never in a single trip. For me, one of the confidence-building aspects of the first round of forty-eight 4,000-footers was that twelve or so miles seemed completely doable. No question. After completing that first hike, I discovered that I'd been right. One of the differences this time around with my friends was certainly going to be the extra mileage that comes with doing two peaks in the same trip.

Some of you may know Chris from my presentations or from *Forward, Upward, Onward*. He was a former employee of mine whose father had passed away from Huntington's disease when he was only in his early fifties. Chris was only nineteen when his dad died. Huntington's is a neurological disease that is potentially hereditary. Chris has a fifty percent chance of having the same genes that will lead to the disease.

Chris and I did many of the 4,000-footers together on my first round of them.

I mention all this because Chris was (and is) about as resilient a human as I've ever met. He's always been up for a challenge in the mountains. But more importantly, he's also up for the topsy-turvy challenges that life can bring.

I look up to Chris in many ways. And I hope that I've been a bit of an uncle or big brother to him. He's been through a lot.

Going back to the White Mountains with him was like old times. We had lots of laughs, and the hike was effortless—all except the three-mile road walk back to the car.

"Our attitude towards life determines life's attitude towards us."

-John Mitchell

Why is it that we can trounce all day up hills, and over rocks and wet roots, but it's the easiest part of the hike that's actually the hardest? I venture to guess that it's because it's the least challenging, the most boring, and certainly the least mindful part of any hike. But overall, that day hiking with Ike, Pierce, and Chris was another lesson in humility and resilience for me. Much of that comes from mindset.

When I'd hiked the Bonds Traverse of New Hampshire with another good friend, Evan, several years ago, I didn't think I was going to complete the hike. The trail leads over six 4,000-foot peaks and is just shy of twenty-three miles. We drove in for the hike separately, and we went early. We car spotted at both trailheads, meaning we both drove to the final trailhead, then took one of the cars back to our starting point.

The hike was arduous to say the least. Often with hiking, just as with life, there are good days and bad days. Sometimes willpower and energy need to be summoned almost magically. And somehow that magic occurs.

We summited the first of the six peaks, and I was wiped out. Emotionally and physically drained. My buddy gave me a pep talk before we started the second peak, South Twin. In my opinion, it offers one of the best views in the whole Northeast. The view helped my morale immensely. What had almost been an aborted hike turned around in just a matter of an hour. Why was that? I propose that much of a hike is all mindset. What you set your mind to can often mean the difference between success and failure. My changed outlook was influenced by the view and trek ahead, but it was also my own choice.

As the hike progressed, the fatigue set back in. The trail is a pretty straight shot over all but one of the peaks: West Bond. It was a simple half mile out to the summit, then the same for the return to the main trail. As we approached the peak, I calmly said I probably wasn't going to make it. My buddy reminded me that if I was going to peak-bag all forty-eight 4,000-footers, I needed this one. We could skip it, but I would have to do another twenty-mile trip to claim it in the future.

What did I do?

I mustered up the fortitude and, more importantly, the mindset to get it summited and checked off of my list. This not a heroic deed by any means. Nor is it a one and done—especially on longer and more difficult hikes. There are many times when I need to dig deeper and deeper to find the motivation and self-encouragement to carry on. Luckily, like any muscle, the power of mindset and attitude gets easier the more you use it.

Perhaps the hardest part of the whole hike was the flat and unassuming Lincoln Woods trail at the end—five miles or so of monotonous walking. And if that wasn't enough, we still needed to bring car #2 to car #1 at the original trailhead we started at to retrieve the other vehicle. We also had to drive the two and a half hours back home that night. We were absolutely exausted.

When it comes to that hike, I was most proud of my mindset shift. That, more than anything else, was the key to getting it done. It was also something I took with me into the real world afterward.

Science is proving that when we think we're done, as in no more gas in the tank, and are ready to throw in the towel, we're really only using about twenty-five percent of our mental and physical capacity. In other words, we still have seventy-five percent left to tackle the obstacle before us. That's a lot left.

Marathon runners often dig deep for the last few miles of their race. Even though they've trained and trained, it's the mental part that really gets the job done. You see, being tired is mostly just a state of mind.

Every day, 60,000 thoughts filter through our brains. Can you fathom that? That doesn't even count being constantly bombarded with advertising and social media. Those 60,000 thoughts are all ours. We make up those 60,000 all by ourselves.

Mentally, you can do more harm to yourself than others can do to you. It's what you allow yourself to think of yourself that really hurts—not what other people say or do.

"You find peace not by rearranging the circumstances of your life, but by realizing who you are at the deepest level."

-Eckhart Tolle

Here's a little trick I learned for putting things into perspective. I wrote about it in *Learning to be Human Again*.

Do you know who you are? Who are you?

Are you your name? Your occupation? Are you your

purpose?

You are none of these.

Maybe you think you're made up of your thoughts.

But actually, you're not those either.

Are you ready for the big revelation?

You are the one who notices those thoughts. THAT'S who you really are.

When you know that, those thoughts don't hold as much power. After all, they're just thoughts. Thoughts are only you ruminating and creating a false reality in your head.

Those thoughts are just chatter. When you notice that chatter, it's easier to gently stop it from taking over your life.

I always imagine that I'm gently sweeping the thoughts out of my ear from inside my head. It's no different from cleaning some dirt or dust off the floor. The visual is powerful for me.

We are not our thoughts. And knowing that opens up another big lesson: We find what we look for in this world. We create that headspace we live in. We can choose the direction our thoughts go in.

Is the concept easy? Yes!

Is it as easy in practice as it sounds? No!

But with practice, we get better.

Most of my practice came through the planned adversity of hiking. Pushing through the lazy and tough days forced me to meet my thoughts and decide to replace them with better ones. And that helped me remember why I was doing all of this to begin with.

Which leads me to this: motivation is overrated. So it's important to work on your why.

Motivation fades. It's easy to hype yourself up, but most of that is fluff. Motivation is convincing yourself to do something when the underlying reason isn't good enough. Work on that reason you do something. Work on your why. When it comes to attitude adjustment, there are many tricks and things you can do to make that easier. Even when I was writing this book, I dragged my feet at some points. So I had to come up with the why.

Your why, regularly reminded and re-visited, can inspire you to finish a goal. If your why isn't strong enough, then maybe it's time to either readjust or scrap that goal altogether. Some goals just weren't meant to be. As the old saying goes, "You can do anything you want in life. You just can't do everything."

"It's not what happens to you, but how you react to it that matters."

–Epictetus

Another of the biggest lessons I've learned on the trail is to work with what I have. The problem isn't always the actual problem, As I've mentioned, it's our reaction to the problem that's the problem. Wishing something away or wishing we had picked a different route or taken this or that with us doesn't solve the obstacle at hand. This is one of the biggest reasons people get lost on the trails: they keep getting themselves in more trouble because they panic. Granted, there are times when immediate action is necessary, but when you accurately assess a situation, you can surmount it much more easily.

I saw a T-shirt recently that read, "Everything is figure-outable." I liked that. Because almost everything does have a solution. That should always be the first reaction: I can figure this out.

Ask any thru-hiker of a major hike, and they'll tell you how they rigged together a ripped pack or boots with duct tape and some string. They adapted. They firmly set their why and made it happen.

A big part of attitude is the ability to adapt. I think many new hikers haven't honed that skill yet. Every time you hear the "How much further?" line, that could probably be translated into "This isn't what I thought it was going to be. This isn't easy or pleasant. I'm going to choose to be miserable."

It's okay to have a bad day (or hike) now and then. We're all allowed. Just don't stay there longer than you have to. Get it out of your system, pick yourself up, and get on with life.

Life isn't always about what's sitting right in front of you. It's often about seeing the possibilities it can offer. See life for not only what it is, but what it can be.

FIND YOUR TRIBE

"We don't accomplish anything in this world alone ... and whatever happens is the result of the whole tapestry of one's life and all the weavings of individual threads from one to another that creates something."

-Sandra Day O'Connor

Surround yourself with good people—with like-minded people, with people who hold the same values you do. Surround yourself with the brave and the kind. The wise and the open minded. With the spiritually minded and the grounded. Surround yourself with good people.

One of the benefits of finding a tribe is the shared experiences you have together. This book uses hiking as a reference point, but think about how many vacations or experiences you've had and were able to share. Don't get me wrong—as an introvert, I love my alone time. I've often vacationed alone. There have been times, however, when I've stood at the Grand Canyon and wished I could have leaned over to a good friend to say, "Wow. Isn't that breathtaking?" Luckily, I have been to the Grand Canyon many times with friends and was able to do just that.

I often equate a big or difficult hike to a battle, and the people I hike with as my fellow soldiers. I say that because many of the big hikes almost feel as though they need to be slayed in some way versus simply hiked. Just like soldiers share camaraderie, so it is with the people you hike with. Many of my fondest memories of mountain climbing have been the most difficult hikes that I shared with those who went with me. Fellow hikers and I often reminisce about climbs we did together twenty years ago. "Remember the time we …" is an important phrase that involves a shared experience. These are often life-changing experiences.

"Those who appreciate the ways of simple tribes, where every activity is direct and immediately understandable, are able to live among them."

-Ella Mallart

I'm lucky. I have several tribes. The good news is that you can have more than one! Chances are you also have more than one.

Another wonderful thing about tribes and shared experiences is that we can easily and gladly celebrate others. When someone needs mentoring for something I've done or encouragement for something they're going to do, I can provide that. Everyone in the tribe can provide that. We know what a hard hike feels like.

We know what a twenty-five-mile day feels like. We can share our knowledge because we share a passion. I can turn to the tribe for guidance and direction. I can lean on them for knowledge. And in turn, they can lean on me.

That's part of what a tribe does.

My writing tribe's moto is "A rising tide lifts all boats." I love that. In a competitive world, you can easily get drawn into keeping information to yourself. Among my writing tribe, it's quite the opposite. We take great joy in seeing the success of others. I know it inspires me to believe I can better myself. I know many of them are making comfortable livings doing what they do (and love). That gives me hope that one day, with hard work, I could be there as well. Someone else paved the path. Sharing that information makes it easier for those coming up.

"One of the marvelous things about community is that it enables us to welcome and help people in a way we couldn't as individuals."

-Jean Vanier

Every year, an important hiking event called Flags on the 48 happens in the White Mountains of New Hampshire. 48 teams of people climb the 48-4,000 foot peaks of New Hampshire and proudly flies an American flag. It commemorates the memory of those lost in 9/11. This event is dear to me for many reasons. First and foremost, I never want to forget what happened to America after 9/11. I also want to honor those who lost their lives on that tragic day. We look too much toward sports figures or entertainment celebrities as heroes or role models. I like to remind myself what a real hero is: The firefighters and police. The passengers on the planes, and the pilots who had no idea what was to come.

Another reason is that the event was one of the first times I realized that hikers are my tribe. I've paticipated in the event seven times, and have made a lifetime of friends through it. So every year, I enjoy meeting new like-minded people and reconnecting with old friends.

This hiking tribe is not quite like anything else I've ever experienced. It's such a close-knit group. Nobody in the tribe cares how much money anyone has, what they look like, or even what their athletic abilities are. It's all about sharing good company in nature. Flags on the 48 reflects those values very much. It has much more to do with the spirit of the memorial than it does with any of the bravado that can be associated with some hikers. Year after year, I keep attending and leading a team for Flags on the 48. Every year I meet someone new or learn something new about someone on our team.

Another of the many benefits of hiking with friends is

that you are spending time together. And I don't mean over-a-cup-of-coffee time. I mean some serious time. You really get to know what someone is made of when you take them up a difficult mountain. The resilient folks shine bright. The others, not so much sometimes. We are also able to spend some considerable amounts of time with one another. Some hikes can take four to six, or even more, hours to complete.

I find that hikers reveal a lot when the blood gets moving and the miles keep passing. The conversation gets looser and deeper. I know that when I'm focused and in my zone, I'm a much better conversationalist. I ask deeper, more intelligent questions, and the mood is generally lighter.

A good friendship or relationship makes both parties better people. I find that those in my hiking tribe are very good people. I've rarely hiked with someone and come back a worse person for it. The few times that has happened—when I came back the worse for wear —I never took the opportunity to hike with them again. It was a well-learned lesson, though. And those are never wasted.

I always hope and strive to make those around me better people. And countless times I know others have made me a better human just by spending quality time with me.

"So many of us feel like we're misfits until we finally find our tribe - the other people who are strange in the same way - and suddenly everything clicks."

-Jenny Lawson

I was once staying on the North Rim of the Grand Canyon. It's a much different experience from the South Rim. Only about ten percent of overall visitors to the Grand Canyon go to the North Rim, so it's a quieter experience. The North Rim is about 1,200 feet higher in elevation, so even though it's only about ten miles across the gap of the Canyon from one rim to another, the landscape and feel of the two rims are different. The North Rim has trees and is grassier, as opposed to the desert and scrub brush of the South. Even the drive in feels different.

I woke in what felt like the middle of the night. Taking a trip out West generally does that to me because of the three-hour time difference. My East Coast body clock thinks five o'clock in the morning in the West is actually eight, which means it's time to get up. Not able to sleep, I figured I would meander to the rim and watch the stars shine and the sun rise over the Canyon. I made my way to the North Rim lodge and was lucky to find that coffee was available that early.

The lodge has an enormous front porch that overlooks the Canyon and is filled with rocking chairs. I sat with my hot coffee and was not disappointed with the show presented to me. There was a thunderstorm moving in about forty miles away, and the streaks of lightning were simply amazing. Living in Massachusetts, I'm not used to a clear line of sight without any obstructions like trees or buildings. The whole storm was happening to my right. Meanwhile, the sky to my left was clear enough to show the sun rising. It was truly an awe inspiring sight.

Something else happened that day that made it even more special though: I was slowly joined by a steady trickle of park employees who'd come to see the same spectacle.

I mention all of this because those employees are part of my tribe. For those of you who are hikers, they are a part of yours as well. But I'd never thought of them as part of my tribe until that morning. These are the folks who clean the rooms or work in the gift shops. They are the waitresses and waiters in the restaurants, and the check-in clerks at the hotels. They're not working these jobs for the money or career opportunities. They work these jobs to see the sunrises and thunderstorms over the Grand Canyon. Most are hikers as well. They endure the barrage of tourists and people every day so that on their off time, they can experience the outdoors and the sheer beauty that surrounds them.

As we sat in awe, we shared an unspoken bond. We weren't the fussy tourists who needed pampering, nor were we the crowd who needed to be held by the hand. We were seasoned outdoors people, gathered to behold a single spectacle together.

After the sun rose and before the rains came in, we started sharing hiking and outdoors stories. "The best sunrise I ever saw ..." "The hardest hike I ever did ..." All those stories started pouring out, and I knew that I was home.

"So managing the community and the tribe; making sure that you're a good member of that tribe, that you're doing your part. When you're around happy inspirational people that are successful, it makes you feel better and you get inspired and if you act on that inspiration, your life will be more fulfilled. And it's not just inspirational in terms of financial success, but in terms of doing difficult things. Whether it's running a hundred miles, which doesn't pay you a lot of money, other than the wealth of the knowledge that you can push yourself to such an extreme. Or anything else, whether it's someone who becomes really good at playing chess, or someone who's really good at martial arts, or whatever it is, there's a great feeling in overcoming these difficult things."

-Joe Rogan

KEEP MOVING FORWARD

Our tribes may not always be obvious when we're out and about in our normal lives, but they're out there. When we start gathering in our places, though, we recognize them. That's when they become more obvious. Writers, knitters, historians, runners, bird watchers, comic book readers, and gamers all have something in common. Their tribe speaks to them like no other. They understand each other like no other tribe can. That's part of the camaraderie.

When it comes to hiking, we light up when we speak with someone else about a trail or peak we've both done. When I talk with someone I've hiked with before, the old hiking stories start coming out in full force.

We all have a slew of guidebooks and maps at our disposal. We know what it's like to not shower for several days, eat packaged energy bars, and boil water on a camp stove for instant oatmeal. We all know what sore feet and rough trails feel like.

I think most of all, we share why we love the outdoors and nature in general. It has a healing property that many people outside the tribe either can't appreciate or have simply forgotten. Tribe members, however, always appreciate and can never forget. We all know someone who started hiking, then couldn't stop. The lure was too strong. They had finally found their tribe.

Look for inspiration in others. Be open to experiencing new people. I've learned much about myself on this journey of life. Much of it, I've learned from others.

KEEP MOVING FORWARD

HIKE YOUR OWN HIKE

"Men and women wander the earth marveling at the highest mountains, the deepest oceans, the whitest sands, the most exotic islands, the most intriguing birds of the air and fish of the sea - and all the time never stop to marvel at themselves and realize their infinite potential as human beings."

-Matthew Kelly

As manager of a small lawn and garden store for almost twenty-five years, I have conducted hundreds of interviews with job applicants. Most of the answers I got didn't actually matter much to me. In most cases, I was just trying to see how a person interacted with me. I wanted to see if they were on their toes or what their personality was like. Dealing with the public isn't always easy, but with the right attitude, it can be a lot of fun. So I was trying to figure out what an applicant's attitude was like.

There was one question, though, that was very revealing. There was no wrong or right answer, but the response said a lot about the candidate. The question was, What is your definition of success? I include this question here, because it ties in very directly with the concept of hiking your own hike.

It's such an open-ended question, but it reveals so much about who you are.

Some candidates said their definition of success was a big house. To others it was making the world better. Many would say that becoming a better person would make them successful.

Again, all of these answers are correct.

At this point, pause and think about that question. What is your definition of success? A sudden answer may come to you. You may also change that answer after contemplation. If you are still trying to discover your purpose in life, this is a key question. The answer to this question may actually be your purpose in life.

So it's a simple but very serious question.

To take it one step further, you can also ask yourself, What is my definition of success for hiking?

The answer to that has changed over the years for me. Why? Because I'm hiking my own hike, and I can do it any way I please.

The initial reason I started hiking was that I wanted to. Plain and simple. Once I got going, I grew and expanded my hiking knowledge. As time went on, I hiked for mental health. As I grew older, I chose specific goals and lists to accomplish. Now that I'm older still, I do it for fun. I simply enjoy hiking. More than I ever have, as a matter of fact. Will this be my final definition of hiking success? Probably not, although all the elements of past definitions are still present.

"It is your road, and yours alone. Others may walk it with you, but no one can walk it for you."

-Rumi

Life is a personal journey. Hiking for me is a personal journey. This may sound obvious to some, but it took me a long time to realize that there's really no right or wrong way to hike.

I don't mean it's not wrong to get lost or not take water. I mean that pace, length, chosen hike, or hiking goals can't be wrong or right. They're personal decisions.

Maybe *definition of success* is an ill way to word it. I think *personal priorities* might suit it better.

You set your priorities and then should examine them often. And they can change over time.

There were times I was unhappy or upset others

because of priorities. When others were peak-bagging and trying to complete certain lists of mountains, I would get frustrated when they said they couldn't hike with me because they had already done that mountain and they needed to do another. Their suggestion to bag another peak was baffling to me because even repeat trips up a beautiful mountain are always worth the effort.

Those people had the power to say no. *No* is a powerful word that can help us in more ways than we think. It frees up time, effort, and much needed energy. That was a power I couldn't understand.

That is, until I started to do those lists myself. THEN I got it. Then I found myself doing the exact same thing: planning hikes around my goal to complete those lists. I solo hiked many, many times to bag peaks. I also hiked with others who knew exactly what completing that list was like and were willing to share the hike and their knowledge with me.

"One of the lessons that I grew up with was to always stay true to yourself and never let what somebody else says distract you from your goals. And so when I hear about negative and false attacks, I really don't invest any energy in them, because I know who I am."

-Michelle Obama

It's important to know not only what your priorities are, but what you are responsible and not responsible for. This is often a huge wake-up call for many.

When I released my first book many years ago, I was pleased that it got some really good reviews. Then one day I got a bad review. That reviewer's biggest complaint was that I'd had the audacity to suggest that we are in complete charge of our own happiness. No one else is responsible for that. I'll assume she was in a bad relationship or had experienced childhood trauma. Still, as tough a pill as it is to swallow, we are in charge of our own happiness.

So in the context of hiking your own hike, let me propose a list of things you are responsible for and a list of things you are not responsible for. The lists may surprise or, in many ways, free you.

You are responsible for:

> Your health
> Your money
> Your actions
> Your responses to challenges or obstacles
> Your happiness
> Your performance at work/school
> Your bad (and good) habits
> Your words
> Your motivation

You are not responsible for:

> Other people's happiness
> Other people's emotions
> Other people's reactions or actions
> Other people's words
> Other people's motivation

You get the picture?

You are responsible for your stuff, and everyone else is responsible for theirs.

You can't manage others' emotions. You also can't save someone else. If you really want to be of use to someone, you can only sit with them to help them through their struggle.

Can other people help with these responsibilities? Can we help others with theirs? Of course! Knowing what's our responsibility and what isn't doesn't mean we can't encourage or be encouraged. We can still help someone be happier or more productive. That's the joy of many of our relationships.

I couldn't have completed or even contemplated many of the hikes I've done without the help of others. It was their encouragement and even just their company that made those hikes possible.

Many of the hikes required long mileage. Many also

required some orienteering. Heck, many just needed advice from someone who had done them before, like what direction to loop or which trails to choose. Hikers told me how much water to carry or warned me about difficult trail conditions. All of this advice was of great help to me.

Ultimately, however, I was responsible for following that advice.

"Comparison is the thief of joy."

-Theodore Roosevelt

The mountains will remind you to stay humble. They will, in fact, humble you if you forget that. Almost any high peak will remind you that you're human and that it is still very much in charge. Mountains often allow us to embrace and participate with them, but very often, they are more than ready to remind us of what we're made of. On some occasions, we risk our lives in order to learn that lesson.

In the fall of 2017, I went to Zion National Park. I'd been there many times before and hiked it a lot. The one trail that always eluded me, though, was Angel's Landing. You see, I'm afraid of heights. Really afraid. And Angel's Landing is a ridgeline, knife-edge hike that's about 3 to 4 feet wide and has a sheer drop of

1,500 feet on each side. This is not a hike for the faint of heart, or the faint of heights. But 2017 was the year I was going to face and beat that fear.

As I pushed my way farther and farther up the trail, it didn't seem so bad. I was really going to do this! The trail started to drop off sharply, but it was tolerable. I could see the summit just ahead of me, and it didn't look as bad as I thought it would. Then, as I came up over the high point, I realized that I had come over a sort of false summit. The REAL hike lay before me. My mouth went dry and I couldn't stop my legs from shaking. There, ahead of me, was the real hike. The sheer drops were obvious, and the elevation gain to the actual end point was very real.

I knew immediately that it wasn't the hike for me. No way, no how.

I had to turn around. My confidence quickly faded.

Was I disappointed? Not really. I knew that this was an easy hike for some people. And I knew that I wasn't one of them. I was okay with that.

I trusted my instincts and listened to my intuition. Your gut usually knows what's going on. As long as you can quiet your head long enough, your instincts will generally shine through. It's tough to quiet the head, though.

In the case of Angel's Landing, how did I know which was my head and which was my gut? My head was obviously shouting the whole way. Like it often does, it was having a two-way conversation, asking and answering all the questions by itself. It was talking about the sure death I would encounter if I attempted the hike while also falsely trying to reassure me that I'd be fine. A lot of "What's the worst that can happen?" talk was going on there.

"If you cannot find peace within yourself, you will never find it anywhere else."

-Marvin Gaye

Many of you may have encountered (or someday will encounter) the same thing on a hike:

"The weather doesn't look good. Should I turn back?"

"I'm not feeling my best."

"That bad knee I have is starting to act up again."

In some of these cases, pressing on is actually the best choice. In other cases, putting pride away and turning back is the correct answer.

We've all heard rescue stories about hikers who not only failed to prepare, but in many cases should have turned back much earlier and licked their wounds back at the trailhead over a cold beer.

The key for me is to stop. I mean physically stop. Then listen. Not for words, but for what I know is right. I often even ask the question, What's the next right thing to do right now? The answer rarely fails me.

We may use the excuse that life is us vs. the world. After all, it's a tough life, right? We're battling our job, our boss, the traffic, a spouse, the kids, and the taxman. It's us against neighbors, relatives, friends, and people on the street.

That's not true, though. Life is ultimately all about you vs. you. That's why hiking a mountain is so rewarding. You really aren't hiking that mountain to conquer it. The mountain doesn't care. It's been there for thousands upon thousands of years and will continue to be there long after we're all gone. The mountain doesn't owe us anything. It's not mad at us or impressed by us in any way.

We don't conquer mountains. What we do when we summit a mountain is conquer ourselves. We learn to push forward to become better people. We conquer our fears, and we realize our dreams and goals. Our sense of accomplishment rises, and we give credence to our hope and faith.

We knew we could do it.

Don't chase people. Do your own thing. Be yourself and work hard. The right people ... The ones that really belong in your life ... will come to you and stay."

-Elon Musk

We can conquer ourselves on so many levels. Everyone has their own mountain to climb. We all have our own definition of what our own personal Everest is. This is ultimately how we hike our own hike. A three-mile hike with 1,000 feet of elevation gain to a new or out-of-shape hiker is Mt. Everest. To someone else, that same hike is a casual walk in the park.

During my talks for *Forward, Upward, Onward*, I would describe my frustration and eventual elation over bagging peaks in the Northeast. I would talk about how proud I'd been over lumbering up what I thought was an excruciating mountain. But more than once, as I explained in those talks, I would meet another hiker on the summit who would innocently ask me, "How many peaks are you doing today?"

How many? Isn't this one enough? I would think.

Of course, I would reply with something like, "Well, I was thinking just this one. You know, as a warm-up. How about you?"

Then they would talk about the third or fourth peak

they'd bagged for the day. You know, a slow day for them.

I would let it get to me sometimes, but I'd work to brush it off. With increased practice, I've also been able to do some multiple-peak hikes, but I usually keep that information to myself.

There was one moment that made up for much of that frustration, though. I was hiking New Hampshire's Mt. Washington, which is often famed for having the worst weather in the world. It's a unique and beautiful climb. With fairly easy access for the general public, it's also extremely busy in the summer and fall. Mt. Washington not only has a famous cog railway that folks can take to the summit, but it also has a road. For a fee, you can drive up the tallest peak in the Northeast. Needless to say, the summit received fewer hikers than folks who had taken transportation of some kind up the mountain.

More than once, wide-eyed tourists asked us hikers if we'd *really* hiked all the way up. A few even took photos with us, as if we had climbed Mt. Everest. It was a perspective changer, to say the least. In those folks' eyes, we were heroes. I heard a lot of people say, "I could never do that. Wow, that's awesome." To us, all we'd done was climb a mountain.

KEEP MOVING FORWARD

"This above all; to thine own self be true."

-William Shakespeare

That Billy Shakespeare was right. We can learn a lot about ourselves and make life a lot easier by just following his advice.

You shouldn't always be afraid of losing other people. You should be more afraid of losing yourself while trying to please other people. With that said, I'm going to continue to release my need for approval or comparison and stick by my firm belief in my ability to change the world with the work that I do.

What I do matters.

You do you.

I'll do me.

EMBRACE THE SACRIFICE

"Life is difficult. This is a great truth, one of the greatest truths. It is a great truth because once we truly see this truth, we transcend it. Once we truly know that life is difficult-once we truly understand and accept it-then life is no longer difficult."

-M. Scott Peck.

Those words from M. Scott Peck in the above quote changed my life.

I'd always been under the assumption that we were supposed to be happy all the time. Or at least striving to be happy. Life was supposed to be easier than it was.

Life is not supposed to be easy.

Read that last sentence again.

Trying to avoid the inevitable challenges and difficulties of life will only compound your suffering.

There, I said it. I ripped the band-aid off. (I hope it didn't hurt too much.)

You don't know that everything is going to be okay

until you confront and walk (or wobble) through the discomfort of life's inevitable difficulties. Until you do that, you will (mostly) only complain and grow in resentment. And that is the REAL killer of joy and serenity.

I know, because I was there for many years.

People often tell me that they wish they could write a book. "Wow, how do you do it?" they ask.

Would you like to know the deep, dark secret? Would you like to know how I magically do it? Are you ready?

I write.

I know. The answer probably was neither worth the build-up nor what you had in mind, but it's the truth.

An acceptable size for a nonfiction book like this one is about 30,000 to 40,000 words. That means that if you write only 444 measly words a day, you could produce a rough draft for a book in ninety days. It would take most folks only about thirty minutes or so to write 444 words. If you wrote 1,000 words a day, you could write a book in thirty days.

It isn't that hard, and it isn't rocket science.

In other words, if you write for only thirty minutes a day, you could write two or three books a year. If you were to just turn off the television or get off social media for a half hour, or wake up thirty minutes earlier, you could write a book. You could write several books in a year, actually.

I've also done some pretty long hikes (for me, anyway). A few years ago, I hiked the Grand Canyon. It was a wonderful but exhausting experience. After I completed it, people asked me, "How did you do it?"

The answer, much like writing, is the same. I just kept walking until it was done.

It wasn't easy, but that's the way it's done. It was just like any other hike: one small step at a time, repeated over and over and over again. I rested often, and I didn't break any speed records. But it got accomplished.

"The person who risks nothing, does nothing, has nothing, is nothing. He may avoid suffering and sorrow, but he cannot learn, feel change, grow or live."

-Leo Buscaglia

The COVID-19 outbreak aside, Americans have never been healthier, more informed, or more socially connected. We have also never been more anxious or depressed. I'm no doctor, but I think much of the mental health decline in the last twenty years or so is due in part to comfort. In this case, I don't necessarily mean comfort zone, but more of a physical and mental comfort. The trouble is, we like feeling comfortable. The problem is that comfort breeds a lack of resilience and grit. We need to push through the bad in order to feel better in the long term. We need to adjust to what bad feels like. In some ways, this process is similar to a mental vaccine. Just like a vaccine against viruses, we need small doses of struggle in order to build up an immunity to it.

When we receive a vaccine against disease, it essentially replicates the disease in a small dose. Your body, in turn, builds up an immunity. That way, if the actual disease attacks, the antibodies are ready to defend. The small dose of the replicated offender helps the body build defense. We are put under stress to make ourselves stronger.

Life events are similar. For example, we never completely get over the loss of a loved one, but as we grow older and more mature, we adjust better to these losses. The same applies to face-to-face social situations. Communication skills improve. We often peel away toxic friendships or relationships.

When I started hiking, I wasn't ready for the challenge of an Everest or Kilimanjaro. I'm still not. But that doesn't mean I can't build up to that point. When I first started hiking, five miles seemed unbelievable. Now, that length is a daily ritual. At first, an elevation gain of a few hundred feet was exhausting. Now, a few thousand feet is common. Not long ago, hiking twenty miles seemed impossible to me. I've since hiked that distance many times. Appalachian thru-hikers often do that every day—in many instances, over the course of five or six months. A twenty-mile hike is a daily ritual for them.

Was getting to that point of hiking twenty miles or gaining a few thousand feet enjoyable? Many times, it was not. It was exhausting. I'm so glad I pushed past those plateaus, though. I may not do many twenty-mile walks these days, but doing those make the ten-mile hikes easier. I built up a tolerance by hiking a mile, then several, then adding elevation to the equation. All the while, an increase in suffering directly equated to an increase in tolerance.

"The most beautiful people we have known are those who have known defeat, known suffering, known struggle, known loss, and have found their way out of the depths. These persons have an appreciation, a sensitivity, and an understanding of life that fills them with compassion, gentleness, and a deep loving concern. Beautiful people do not just happen."

-Elisabeth Kübler-Ross

We are taken into troubled waters not to drown, but to

be cleansed. Facing life through the struggle and the difficulties actually doesn't make life any easier, but it does make us stronger. It's our strength and hope that carry us forward.

There's an old prayer that goes, "Lord, don't offer me an easy life, but the ability to face it all well with strength and dignity."

The important thing is not the triumph, but the struggle. There is incredible value in the struggle.

How many mountains have I climbed, gasping for air and pushing my legs harder than I'd like to? How many times did I wish the hike were over sooner? How many miles have I put my head quietly down and just kept pushing through the mental fatigue?

Too many to count.

With that said, how many times after completing any of those hikes was I elated that I'd gone the distance?

Almost all of them. I regretted many hikes in the midst of them, but I regretted few after they were done.

As I get more accustomed to these adventures, my physical and mental resilience grow considerably. I know what to expect now. I can calm my mindset and forge forward.

This methodology is well suited to life. The more I've suffered (I use that term loosely) on the trails, the easier almost all other aspects of my life have become.

The less comfortable I've made myself, the better able I am to adapt to the curveballs life has thrown at me. Suffering holds power, both good and bad. When you triumph over it, you take away its power to control you. If you're not afraid to get wet, muddy, or hungry, you start to build resilience. You begin to feel more confident. Pretty soon, by getting wet and cold and hungry and making your way through it, you're standing up for yourself and others more. You find yourself asking for that raise or setting long-needed boundaries. You start to realize that life's small daily challenges aren't that big of a deal. Maybe you were the kind of person who had a bad five minutes and stretched it out all day. Or maybe the hundred little distractions and annoyances of the day really got under your skin. But when you face yourself and those annoyances, you calm the nature of them. You take away their power.

"Some people dance in the rain, others just get wet"

-Bob Marley

I feel bad for the folks who are afraid to get wet in the rain and get their feet a little muddy. I also feel bad for those who think jumping in a puddle is senseless. We are connected to all of it. We need to feel the rain.

For years, I was afraid of getting my feet wet by falling into a stream while crossing it. I equated that water to molten lava. One day, I was hiking with a friend who simply stopped at the stream's edge, removed her boots and socks, and crossed the stream barefoot. Upon seeing the smile on her face mid-stream, I decided to do the same. The experience was pure bliss. I felt like a carefree child again. My fear and mindset about water crossings changed almost immediately.

Making myself uncomfortable by getting wet on purpose made the journey easier and changed my attitude completely. It was just water. Why was I so petrified to fall in?

Quite honestly, it wasn't really even an uncomfortable situation. I literally took off my socks and boots, then just walked through the stream. I say it made me feel like a kid again, because that's what we did as kids, right? No one could keep us away from stuff like that. Jumping in puddles, playing in the water—it was all a great joy.

Then life programmed us to think differently. Actually, we programmed ourselves to think differently. It was no longer fun. Then it almost morphed into danger. That's when we learned to think, *I'm about to have a potentially uncomfortable situation! Retreat!*

Granted, when I say I did a stream crossing, I'm not talking about walking through a rushing river in 33-

degree weather. Those are genuinely dangerous situations. I crossed the stream on a warm, dry day.

Getting muddy, wet, hungry, and cold all have something in common: they all make us uncomfortable. But we need to feel discomfort. Why? Because we need to push through the other side of discomfort to gain the reward. Our uncomfortable situation will soon turn around. There will eventually be another side to it: the warm bed, the hot meal, the cold beer, or the dry clothes. We need to experience the discomfort to appreciate the comfort.

People have been touting the benefits of meditation for years because it supplies us with that discomfort in a small burst. As I mentioned, these small, planned bursts of struggle are the building blocks for larger, more significant improvement.

Meditating is the easiest principle in the world and also one of the hardest to follow: concentrate on your breath and stop thinking. Simple, but so not simple.

During meditation, we experience minor back or neck pain. We have an itch but can't scratch it. We lose track of our breath, and our thoughts wander. These are all small, planned adversities. Believe it or not, by slowly and carefully training our brains to ignore the itch, or compassionately drawing our thoughts back to something as basic as our breath, we are facing small trials and tribulations. The overcoming of these small inconveniences carry through to our everyday lives. This practice helps us strengthen the discipline we need so badly.

Here's the easiest way I can describe discipline. This makes more sense to me, and perhaps will make more sense to you:

Easy choices = hard life

Hard choices = easy life

That's it.

"Let us never look hardship in the face and run. To do so tears   ourselves from this world and this time, and to relinquish our growth and contributions in life"

-Brendon Burchard

I have a saying that I use frequently: You pay now, or you pay later. But sooner or later, you have to pay.

Did you make sacrifices early in life to save for retirement? Did you sacrifice for your physical and mental health? For your relationships?

None of those are easy. Many people waited too late and are paying now. Many made the sacrifices early and are enjoying the fruit now.

I'm not saying that there is a right or wrong way. Many sacrificed early for retirement then passed away before they could enjoy the fruits of their labor. I think there needs to be a balance, but some struggle is certainly necessary early in life in order to prevent an overwhelming struggle later.

Discipline is a dirty word to some. It certainly was to me for years. *Sacrifice* is another dirty word to many. Sacrificing precious time and energy to apply discipline isn't too high on most people's to-do lists. It is, however, the means to becoming successful. It's how goals are accomplished. Discipline and sacrifice drive us up our mountains.

Discipline is what helps us focus. It keeps us on the path to our destination. It keeps us away from distractions.

Are you having difficulty achieving your goals? Is your world filled with distractions? Don't blame your distractions. Instead, improve your focus and be willing to feel uncomfortable for a while.

What lessons have you learned through your personal adversity?

Life isn't easy, but I wouldn't have it any other way

KEEP MOVING FORWARD

"If you can't fly, then run. If you can't run, then walk. If you can't walk, then crawl. But whatever you do, you have to keep moving forward."

-Martin Luther King Jr.

There are so many other lessons I could have subdivided this chapter into, but I came to the conclusion that many fell under one category: Keep Moving Forward. This was the most important of all the lessons I've learned on the trails and in life for so many reasons.

This theme covers discipline, resilience, grit, and determination. Of all the lessons, these were the biggest factors in my overall growth—not only as a hiker, but as a human. These qualities trickled down to all the others. Discipline and determination helped my attitude. Grit built my confidence. And resilience slowly whittled away my fear.

I posed this question earlier, but it bears asking again: How do you eat an elephant? The answer, of course, is one bite at a time.

How do you climb a mountain? One step at a time.

How do you get through life? One minute or one day at a time.

Many, many times, especially on longer hikes, I would sing the refrain of a song from the 1970 Christmas claymation special "Santa Claus Is Comin' to Town." It cheerfully resounds with, "Put one foot in front of the other, and soon you'll be walkin' out the door." I would repeat over and over as a mantra: *Just one more step. Just one more step…*

People often ask me for my secret to getting through depression. My answer is not always an expected or popular one. It is, however, simple: go through the depression and do the work. The same applies to anything in life.

"When you're going through hell, keep going."

-Sir Winston Churchill

The work at hand may need to be reading; seeing a therapist; talking to a friend; exercising; watching videos on pertinent topics; and learning more about the science of the brain, as well as causes of or remedies for your condition. Doing these things is not an instant fix, of course, but it is forward motion. That motion alone is imperative. Doing the work is as well.

It's no different from climbing a mountain: maintain forward motion and do the work.

Mountains won't climb themselves, and nobody can climb one for you. The Grand Canyon was formed over millions of years by running water eroding the walls of the Canyon around it, one drop at a time. Hiking is no different. One step at a time.

Drip, drip, drip … Step, step, step …

Another important part of doing the work is holding yourself accountable. Nobody will do the work for you, and nobody can necessarily make you do it, either. That isn't to say that we can't surround ourselves with loving and supportive people who can encourage us as much as possible. That certainly helps. But the work, and equally the why behind it, is all yours.

A few years ago, after climbing Mt. Garfield in New Hampshire, I decided to try something I had never done before: hike a 4,000-footer two days in a row.

But as it turned out, I wasn't ready for that second peak. I had to turn back.

Earlier in the day, as I started the second hike, a group of younger folks were assembling to do the same trip. On my way down, after deciding I couldn't finish the hike, I realized that the old Matt would have thought I was doing a walk of shame. The old Matt would have wondered, *What would those kids think of me now?* On my way down, I had to pass them as they were coming up the trail. The old Matt would have been bothered by the idea that those kids would think I was a quitter or that I couldn't handle the hike. The new Matt didn't care. And the kids didn't care, either. As a matter of fact, I had to encourage a few of them who were having a hard time early in the hike.

It's also important for me to note that this was the first 4,000-footer I ever turned away from because I just physically couldn't do it. Was I disappointed? Hell no. I was elated!

I'd tried something I couldn't do, but I knew where my limitations lay and what I needed to do to get to a point where I could do peaks back to back.

Mind games are a dangerous thing sometimes. To me, even going down a mountain is still moving forward. Even when I'm turning back from one.

Quarterbacks have a neat trick that I incorporated into my life for a period. They place a rubber band around their wrist. After a horrible play, they gently snap the rubber band to condition themselves to forget it and move onward with the next play. That helps them develop the ability to shake off the last play and focus on the next. They learn to keep the past in the past.

In the 2004 American League playoffs, the Boston Red Sox were down three games to none against their archrivals, the New York Yankees. The Red Sox had stopped focusing on the past and focused instead on what lay ahead. They just needed to win the game at hand. Then they needed to win the game at hand, then they needed to win the game at hand. The odds were certainly stacked against them. No team had ever come from behind to win after such a large deficit, ever.

Still, they didn't concentrate on that. They just needed to win the game they were playing, one inning at a time. The Red Sox ended up defeating the Yankees by winning the next four games in a row. They went on the win their first World Series in eighty-six years. The eighty-six-year curse was finally over.

I mentioned earlier the epiphany I experienced through these simple, but profound words from M. Scott Peck in his book *The Road Less Traveled*:

Life is hard.

That one simple statement was earth shattering to me. It still is. For years I had been under the impression that I could eliminate sadness or pain from my life. This one sentence gave me the permission to stop fighting myself. I could stop trying in vain to rid myself of these necessary lessons. The energy I was spending trying to push away the hard stuff had left me exhausted. And guess what? None of it was going away. It wasn't until I embraced these critical lessons that I really started growing and began to experience a fuller life.

The army has a great way of putting it. embrace the suck.

I'm often reminded of perseverance when I see what seems to be the impossible scenarios of plants and full-size trees growing on top of rocks, where they shouldn't be. I marvel at roots reaching downward toward the earth, and the tall tree suspended magically above the boulders, perched above it as if that's exactly and comfortably where it needs to be. The tree seems to know its place and, more importantly, it isn't giving up anytime soon. You often see that even in urban areas, where weeds grow in the small cracks in asphalt and concrete. I admire the tenacity of these plants. Of nature. If we think about it, we're not much different. We're hardwired to survive. This hardwiring is often a muscle that needs to be worked out, though. The more resilience we exhibit, the easier life becomes.

"Funny the difference a year can make, right? Not just on a hike, but in our lives as well. Have you ever had a miserable season or year? Cold and unsure? Then a year later you look back and it's like you're thinking about a different person and situation altogether. A year can make a big difference. For that matter, a day can also make a big difference. I've often gone to bed worried and frustrated from the day, only to wake up the next morning refreshed and ready to fight the battle anew."

-Excerpt from Forward, Upward, Onward

KEEP MOVING FORWARD

Taking one step back and two steps forward is still forward motion in the long run. I'd argue in most cases that the one step back is still a step forward, though.

When I was promoting *Forward, Upward, Onward,* I gave dozens of presentations on the lessons I've learned on the hiking trail. The first lesson was to never look back —that is, unless you're looking back to see how far you've come.

I guess we don't really feel forward motion unless we know we're going forward. By seeing the progress we've made in a constructive way, we can hold onto hope. We know that we can continue in a forward motion.

I mentioned this earlier, when I made my first trip up the bigger peaks of New Hampshire, I was with two friends, and we were horribly unprepared. We could have easily come into harm's way on that trip. We'd taken no extra food or water, were underdressed, and started too late.

We were hiking the iconic Lincoln/Lafayette Loop, which encompasses three peaks along a breathtaking ridgeline. It's about a ten-mile hike with several thousand feet of elevation gain. A somewhat monumental task for three beginners.

There was a point where we were approaching the third peak and it was starting to get dark. We had no sources of light with us, and finishing the hike didn't feel very hopeful. We were exhausted and dejected. As we summited the last peak, we could see the ridge that was to take us back to the trailhead. The length of it looked un-hikeable. At that point, I turned around to see how far we'd already come. We'd already done over two thirds of the arduous journey. The long ridgeline that we had already hiked was visible behind us. A sudden flow of hope seeped into me. The scowl on my face began to turn into a faint smile. We were going to be okay. By looking back, I could see that what lay ahead was nothing compared to what we had achieved that afternoon.

"Every mountain top is within reach if you just keep climbing."

-Barry Finlay

Every path leads two ways. When walking the same path back, you often get a sense of victory. The path not only looks different from how it looked when you were going the other direction, but it also feels different. You're often tired and beat up. Sometimes muddy and drenched in sweat. But you feel victory in your bones. You may feel beaten in some ways, but you really know, deep down, that you're not.

"If you only walk on sunny days, you'll never reach your destination."

-Paulo Coelho

We're often too hard on ourselves. Life can be messy, and we can all be less than perfect. Life hands us problems that need to be faced and dealt with regularly. By creating a sort of planned adversity, we can adjust and expand our comfort zones little by little. Mountain by mountain.

So how can we gain the fortitude, wisdom, and resilience we need? There are a variety of things we can do, but I'll stand behind climbing mountains. The more physical mountains we climb, the easier it becomes to deal with the hypothetical mountains of life.

By letting the world disappear for a little while and putting our heads down to tackle something difficult, we build grit—even if it's a struggle we created. We build the mental and physical muscle needed to forge on. We prove to ourselves that we can successfully face adversity in our attitudes, mindset, relationships, and everyday life.

Maybe more important than anything else, we also increase our capacity for hope. We realize the future isn't as bad as we make it out to be. The view from the top of the mountain, after all the pain and effort, is almost always worth it. The rush we get from the exhilaration of climbing is always worth it.

Life isn't easy, but that doesn't mean we can't rise above that fact. It doesn't mean we can't overcome adversities and obstacles.

We learn that the bumps and struggles of life are what make it worthwhile. By examining ourselves more closely, we grow. And when we grow, we help others do the same.

Hiking creates an empowering alternative in which we can test our physical and mental limits. Interrupting disruptive or destructive patterns is key to forming better habits. Hiking helps interrupt those patterns.

Those who hike know there's a rhythm to the steps. A methodical timing that is much the same as concentrating on your breath while meditating. There's a stillness, yet there's also a vibrancy in your brain. The sights, scents, and sounds are enough to occupy busy minds. The challenge of crossing a river, scrambling on a slide, and butt-dragging to ease yourself down off a small ledge build determination. Climbing the mountain is optional. Coming down is mandatory. We find the way to make it up, and we find a different way to complete the task.

Many of us live lives of regret about the things we wish could have been and choices we wish we could have made better.

KEEP MOVING FORWARD

All that is gone though. The quality of our lives doesn't lie behind us. It lies before us. New choices can be made, some wrongs can be righted, and we can have a new vision for our lives every morning.

Take charge of your own destiny. It is never too late to become who you thought you should have become. You are not a victim. You are empowered. You need to remind yourself of that often. Stop giving away your power.

If you're having regrets about the past, move forward.

If you're climbing a mountain, move forward.

If you're in a difficult time in your life, move forward.

Keep moving forward, because your strength is far, far greater than your struggle.

Made in United States
Troutdale, OR
06/27/2024

20864545R10066